THE PACIFIC NORTHWEST POETRY SERIES

Linda Bierds, General Editor

Charming Gardeners

POEMS *by* DAVID BIESPIEL

UNIVERSITY *of* WASHINGTON PRESS
SEATTLE AND LONDON

*Charming Gardeners, the fourteenth volume in the Pacific Northwest Poetry Series,
is published with the generous support of Cynthia Lovelace Sears.*

Printed and bound in the United States of America
Design by Ryan Diaz
Composed in Scala, designed by Martin Majoor, and Avenir, by Adrian Frutiger
16 15 14 13   5 4 3 2 1

University of Washington Press
PO Box 50096, Seattle, WA 98145, USA
www.washington.edu/uwpress

Library of Congress Cataloging-in-Publication Data
Biespiel, David, 1964–
  [Poems. Selections]
  Charming gardeners : poems / by David Biespiel.
      pages ;   cm. — (The Pacific Northwest poetry series)
  ISBN 978-0-295-99328-7 (cloth : alk. paper)
  I. Title.
  PS3552.I374A6 2013
  811'.54—dc23

                    2013015750

The paper used in this publication is acid-free and meets the minimum requirements
of American National Standard for Information Sciences — Permanence of Paper for
Printed Library Materials, ANSI Z39.48–1984.∞

FOR MY BROTHERS

ALSO BY DAVID BIESPIEL

POETRY
The Book of Men and Women
Wild Civility
Pilgrims & Beggars
Shattering Air

PROSE
Every Writer Has a Thousand Faces

EDITIONS
Long Journey: Contemporary Northwest Poets
Artists' Communities

Let us be grateful to people who make us happy; they are the
charming gardeners who make our souls blossom.

MARCEL PROUST

And when some day dogs chasing a bear
Burst into a crevasse and people of far-off generations
Decipher our angular letters on the wall—
They will be amazed that we knew so many of their own joys,
Though our futile palace has come to mean so little.

CZESLAW MILOSZ

Many such eves of gently whisp'ring noise
  May we together pass, and calmly try
What are this world's true joys, —ere the great voice,
  From its fair face, shall bid our spirits fly.

JOHN KEATS

But Hell, I do like to write letters. Much easier than writing books.

EDWARD ABBEY

CONTENTS

*

*

*

Charming Gardeners

TO _____ FROM THE JEWISH CEMETERY
IN WILLIAMSON, WEST VIRGINIA

Dear _____

      Up from the ground the insistent murmurs that follow us
Not with music or waves of melodies or prayers for the dead
But something that remains through the murk—

                                   sometimes silent and weak,
Sometimes humming and vibrant—a sweet sweet nothing
That's invisible and frivolous and tattered without contempt.
Up from the ground the rumpled tailor and the corner shoe man
With all their knowledge of white feet and the thighs of the living,
Up the haberdasher, up the barkeep, up the founder of Sloan's Mens Store
And the Sisterhood gossips and synagogue gardener
Who sat with the dead from midnight until dawn
Along with the shtetl-fearing dogs with their dark eyes.
Up from the ground the buyers and sellers, the sellers and buyers

                              who fear everyone can be bought,
Who recognize themselves only on Friday nights at linen tables
With silver candlesticks, like two herons, set in the center of the room
As if in the center of God's eye, dovening and benching without hope.
But they don't recognize themselves here.

                        Or I don't.
And yet here is the peddler and the rabbi's friend,
Abe the bookkeeper and Doris his wife, mother of four,
Whose kugel is filled with the yellow platitudes of raisins,
And Ruth come in from the fields of coal
To cook soup and biscuits for her daughters and their men.
She stands on one foot and then the other in the apartment
Across the street from the Mountaineer Hotel,
Flipping the black hair from her eyes,
Stirring the pan, listening to them press up the stairs,
Birds, crickets, a rattle of windows against the sills—

                                    can you hear? —
All of it a little heroic, the great balance and terrible joy.
And three times an hour the townsfolk stopping at the tracks for the coal trains
On their exodus from the mines to the train yards to the electrification plants —
From Williamson to Wheeling, from Wheeling to shining sea,
Coal keeps the lights on.
Coal, coal, like a vaudevillian joke, slightly ridiculous, slightly disturbing,
                                    clanging all day and night.
Coal, coal, with the Atlantic on one side and the Pacific on the other
And Lvov and Cherno Ostrov and Belsen shimmering in between.
Coal, coal, with the little apartments lit up on the Lower East Side,
And gentlemen's farms lit up in Charlottesville,
And the barns of snowy Elma in northern Iowa
                                    lit up even on Saturday mornings
Where inside their kitchens the chipped cups rattle on the shelf in a sudden wind,
The chipped cups unenvied and trustworthy and following us all the way.
Lit up across the prairie gaps between Cheney and Boulder.
Lit up on the islands cramped between Bellingham and Los Angeles.
And lit up in the new housing in the sands of Scottsdale.
Train car after train car with its grave-mounds of coal
And the coughing of America up ahead with its flashing red lights
                                    and sermons against failure —
All the night shirts sleeping around the night bodies,
All the hair nets sleeping around the heads,
And the day lilies from last summer vanishing in the blind dark.
Henry Longfellow's Hebrews are scattered now among the nation
But none of that is really worth our looking for the grounds of the dead
Wherever it might have been, in autumn, here, in overcast Williamson
Because we're carried on the highway and magnified by promises from within —
It's like snow clinging to the lungs. Like snow clinging to the hollows.
Snow clinging to sweetness and nothing and fingers in the dirt,
Into endless swirls across the counties, and the wind picking up
As if to sing into my ear as we press up Highway 52 E
Under the red-leafed canopies of trees —

4

Canopies of the dying, canopies of the dead—
Crisp ruined hearts on the last gold edges of the branches,
An All Hallows grunt, a little sigh, and now, singing in my ear,
                              Where have you gone, Zvi ben Yosef,
Who swept the wooden floors at Zeitman's before school?
Where have you gone, Shlomo ben Yitzhak, who remains unknown
In between tours of duty in Korea and later settles in Kansas City?
                              Where have you gone,
Rivka and Esther, sisters who slept in the same settle bed
Every day of their life until their wedding nights?
I watch the CSX Lines slump in their long dresses,
Braided, and aproned, and bulky,
                              out of one century and into this one,
And I look for the Honorable Robert C. Byrd,
                              who slept in the Mountaineer Hotel
Same as I have, same as Jack and Hubert and Lyndon,
Same as Uncle Reuben and Aunt Rose,
And George and Thomas and James and Abraham.
                              Coal, coal, there, there—
Like the ceaseless whistling of a breeze through the opened windows
Flickering the candle lights above a single shabbat
In the year of who knows when,
All of it faded, all of it nothing in this life
But quiet and proclamation and brick siding.
And the child who has just learned to walk hums against the tepid air.
And the child who has just learned to look out the window
Crawls into a weightless future
As if to be unborn
        and waits for the centipedes of trains
To pass into a beauty of thoughtlessness.
And off in the eastern hollows of Mingo County,
Where I drive on the blacktop of Highway 52 E,
The families of miners fish the orange-watered creeks
                              as if it could be otherwise.

The uncircumcised helpers of light cramped into the hills
Two thousand and eleven years since the birth of Jesus,
Eyes swollen with traces of ash and nicotine and false pregnancies
And vapors of the buried bodies, lamplight after lamplight of tree leaf
And wind flame and the walls dented and the roofs trodden down
And the little bridges across the creeks
Like honeycombs of bones,

                      trampled on, blackened,
Like Yom Kippur clothes are blackened with zippers and buttons
                                and small handkerchiefs
So unlike the bedazzled blue curtains of the holy ark
With its replicas of exodus and betrayal and the spleen of Solomon
Now shuttered and locked in the coal-fired heating systems of the scroll.
                        And now, driving a few miles on into Mingo County,
We've disappeared inside the clouds huddling over the hills
And with the hills huddling over our eyes
Somewhere between Red Jacket and Northfork.
We've disappeared among the lost tribe of the morning sunlight,
Breathing for calm, clenched and crouching,

                        up the highway
All the way through the steeped switchbacks.
And for 70 miles, in every quarter-after-pinched-quarter mile,
The inches of flat land are squeezed into
By nine hundred trailers

        with the hills won or lost
And the dead with no more right to vote,
And the cruddy corrugated steel settling into the ground
Among the clapboard one-storeys
And curb stores and gas pumps,
And not one grocer,
In curve after curve of the pleated hills,

                    not one stick of celery
Or tempered tomato,
Not one handful of peanuts or pop box,

Starved turn after starved turn on the road,
Like a blind diaspora —
All of it with an ungentle weariness that gets to you
And to which you can never ask a single question
                         about vanity or geology.
While under the clouds, there are the fragments of unpiled trees,
Under the clouds, the trampled and checked sheets
And human hair and the torn earth back out of sight,
And the God-made rivers teetering with a heron here
                         and a heron there,
Like tiny flames to stop the flashing hill-light of the day.
I keep looking because I know I'll never get back here.
It's like dying, done once with the tremor of a wound,
A carving, an inscription on the forehead,
A last letter for all the abominations done in the midst.
But the cramped bodies in the deep hollows of the crouched hills
                         refuse to be bloodied.
They remain in the hills like blasted tunnels
And never — and here I'm guessing — travel far away
                         into the tranquility of longing to return
With all the worshippers to home, to a table, a chair,
The good dog lifting its head onto your lap, chin on your thigh,
Looking upward in anticipation
As you put a hand again and again across the rib cage,
And the autumn light owl-like against the yellow trees.
The gall of gnats swarms, too, weaving above the porches
Like the swish from childhood to unreliable beauty to all or nothing
To gray shades of the mountain to death bed.
                         I should stop back there
And stand on both feet in the grazing sunlight
And hear this chorus of America singing.
But I am so afraid of the testament of the delivered.
So we drive onward on Highway 52 E
And rush into all that is not enough,

Past the blind drunks and roughnecks
                              and the small bones,
Past the absent delusions and the early sunsets,
And the football fields crimped with bad knees against the hills,
And the yards of primary schools and worksheets.
We drive and we drive, past the metal swing sets
                              and the uncrumpled fists,
And the six windows on the blue house outside Ennis
Wiped clean by a man on a ladder,
And past whoever he turns out to be,
For that moment, with the road spiraling
And dovetailing through the lost, silent, tribal air,
And all of us, lost or found or looking,
                              falling through ourselves,
Turns out to be nothing more than quarreling with death,
Fairly ordinary, capturing the signals of the chimney sweeps
That sharpen and bawl into the withered branches
Too far from Williamson to get back, too far to live
                              with the sunken, half-sleeping bodies
Gliding shut into the graves,
Train after train, passersby for once,
Into the black drifts of evenings and mornings, and out of history,
Mordecai and Etta and Benjamin and Uncle Eedle and Auntie Leah,
All come out of the year of forgetting into the year of burning —
                              coal, coal,
With its hole-in-the-wall clothes and High Holiday prayer shawls,
With its sooty amens and child's play of resurrections,
With its great halls of dreams
                    and small lightbulbs of the remembered,
Coal, coal, up from the ground into lovingkindness,
Into names of the great-grandmothers
                              and reunions with birth,
The souls of birthplaces like the souls of wishes,
Of sons, and sons of sons, who live to set a single stone on the earth.

TO WENDY FROM YELLOW HICKORY

— Portland

My dear —
        The last pennies I draw from my pocket
Have never been enough. And there are sunsets
Like this one, with the near trains crooning,
That as I hunker under the grapevine
I think I will die in just this sort of swarthy light.
The glory bower I pulled down this morning in the east garden
Came into my hands with savage beauty, and in easy stages.
I sliced the top twigs then set to sawing the base.
Hacking like that is a rehearsal of fear, I know,
Or one way to unrehearse a life.

                                Now the limbs are scattered
Like details on the browning grass. I think even the air
Is uncertain about it, and bleary. I had come to think
It was a bad sign, cutting down the glory bower.

                                Now I'm not so sure.
Suffering is the cost for love.
I've been thinking about other late blights I've handled —
One began with wildflower beds, took over the cosmos,
Walled them in, so that walling, then swollen,
There was nothing blossoming left to parse.
That year, too much fog had something to do with it.
It's too much July now,

                        too much drained out of me to replant.
Sometimes I think being so lovelorn

                                we're late blights, too —
Nervous, moody, spare as jaspers, good for jaywalking,
Sure as shrews with our neighborly cheer and rash work.
And you, so rooted in hunger and tongues —
There are nights you're like a groundsheet,

Dewy and wan, rising up as a ghost.

                          It's foolish, yes, to think this
(And I know learned fools exceed all fools). The worst part of it
Is that for a moment, with you away and the light going,
My heart suddenly was absent of sorrow. But before I went on
To you just now about the old blights, I was going to raise my head
Away from the quick stars that have come on, precise as a woman,
Or as doves, or as what I think dying in bed is like — and I was going
To see if any of the figs had come in out of their dark rooms,
Such soft, bright, silly vibrations of figs.
It doesn't matter, my dear. The time is the time. Soon
They'll fall to the ground with plenty and enough.

TO PLUMLY FROM LUMMI ISLAND

— Washington

Dear Stan —

      You'd have a kick here with the flickers,
What with their gooey squawking for dreamers
And their suits and chubbiness about rainless air
And bad feelings. (Though the bad feelings part is mine.)
The heebie-jeebies are coming on again this time of year.
And the good gin, too — divine gin, pumped up gin.
I know, when the days get weather-beaten
We'll all switch to the cheaper stuff. The impressionists
Can't trump that. To get here, Stan, we passed three dozen
Fireworks stands at the Reservation.

                            One bare-chested honcho
The size of the Duke in a John Ford western,
With an open-heart scar was petting a yellow
                         three-legged kitten.
He was whistling at the pockmarked jays
And winking at the kids feeding rocks to the bay.
That's a spot of time I won't forget, nor this one:
I wished words into that dude's mouth that said: *A master*
And a great love will take a fallen man far.
I know a man should not love rocks too much
Nor let his garden overgrow with rotting gourds,
Nor be unkempt in speech with words
That are softly dear to his heart, words
Like: *lilacs, America, love, ladder, blood.*
Just now I heard an island woodpecker wish
Something similar against one of the taller piney things.
Most nights since we arrived here the wind has been in a havoc,
Has torn at the gate and sent the far tides into a dither, wrecked
The way sleep works. I dreamed this morning such

Fears as hummingbirds must feel, and thought that, had
Even one come close to my lips, I would have said
Sweetheart, kiss me. But even I know
When a thief kisses you, you'd better count your teeth.
(Watching the mainland from here, you get to be making oaths
Like that about seasons, about love, about teeth.
So saith I). Wendy keeps leaping up for the rippled
Tanagers and their yellow heads.

                What I see: a soaked
Blur against the haze. That's nothing new.
We'd like to go on like this, Stan, but posthumously living uphill
From one life, and nearly reborn into the next, is taking its toll.
The waves keep coming up from the bottom of the bay, then fall.
Through the windows we can't see any of our children.

                  Not sure when the ferry leaves.
At the dock coming over, we met a Reservation girl
About three who told us her grandmother lives near the bingo.
She had cut her toes on some glass in the high grass along the beach, too.
Cute girl, a big toothless smile. She was true
As 200 years of dumb government can get us.

                      It's madness,
Stan, what we've done to our kind, but we still love the birds.
My list is short. Not so good, really, beyond a crow.

TO HUGO FROM SODO

— Seattle

Dear Dick—
      The new ball field brought the city hope
At the beginning of the twenty-first century
But hasn't been filled in a while. Surely the plan
Was to win. I mean, the great Japanese right fielder can't save
A whole town with just 200 singles a year!
So I drive on, as you would have,
Bookended with bonhomie and thoughts of home,
And thinking about writing letters to smithereens.
I know I must ask your permission to carry it off.
Or carry it on. Without your postal stacks, I'm no one.
Anyway: The banner clouds here cluster and block
                            and cream the sun,
And the cowbirds crowd the dirt-cheap monuments,
Pecking at dribs. This city's hubbub is barely a saga.
True, some years back, I read in your poems
Something about sailor's knots
And half-tapped kegs
And wished we'd shared a trailer home
                    long enough to sing:
The old gray mare she ain't what she used to be.
Not ten times running, but fifty!
Roethke said it's a town of toothy dames.
Dick, this city is gigantic now—
                    cuffed up, whinnying, off center,
And everyone knows that some night, during sleep,
We'll all die or just come through.
Earlier as I drove past the sputtering
Willows and small fields,
I wanted to trust the shafts of shadows

As if they were dreamed into my head
By a single-minded pent-up God.
The road is that wild with cracks of wind
From one lane to the next.
                    I wonder:
Could I amuse you with my caustic tongue—mull
Nothing worth asking, asking for nothing?
Such notes from one troubadour to another—
(A bit rickety on their little stalks, I know that.)
Still, some days I pray I'll get caught
Inside the scatter of light
And inside every votive mossy name.
What'd you say, Dick? A future of winners?
Do you just need a good pitch to hit?
Don't worry. I'll keep a weather eye out for our kind.

TO BIESPIEL FROM SCHUL

— Portland

Dear brother—

      Just now through their Yad Vashem teeth and holy-holy jowls
Came the survivors to belt out the "Adon Olam" with all the farewell
Sadness they can muster—and the women, too, dolled up
In their Erector Set make-up jobs, and the goody-goody men
Burbling like newborns—not one refugee here reigns supreme.
And the half-decent bubbes, and the tabloidesque light,
And the ushers that are always in vogue
With their sweet *nyack-nyack*:
I've taken their business and fashioned it into a sugary gab,
Until, suddenly, in the middle of it all,
With the full spillage of God, down came the Über rain
Plunking the stained glass and the aging,

                          so-so Romanesque tiles.
Brother, the local Rebbe has just buried his 30-year-old son,
And the Rebbe's wife says he cries at night in his sleep.
I remember the last time you and I sat in schul together,
You said: *If He was, then He is.*
I said: *Infant. Crook.*
But today, I'm as unhappy as ever with the crappy grays
And strung-out nationalist's blues
And lack a hard fear of the Almighty—

                         so, not much has changed.
What I mean is: I admit I was drifting during the mourner's kaddish
And got lost in dull lust for the young bride
Two rows up during the prayer thanking God
For not making me a woman.
I can't say I'm not ruminating at all about faith,
But if the notion entertains itself in my dozy mind,
It's like Groucho winking, "Here is a viaduct to the mainland,"

And Chico saying, "Why a duck? Why-a no chicken?"
And Groucho again, "I don't know. I'm a stranger here myself."
But then I shake with a sally, thinking, boy, am I the bub!
Why a horse? Why a ford? Why a chicken?
Because, all in all, brother, not one thing's a disaster.
I mean, even now, outside the schul,
The mayor is waiting to rattle the jewelry.
Who's to say who among us is the profiteer?
I doubt you'll see me much at the morning service after this one.
To this, surely, mother will say something
About my not sulking during the mourner's kaddish after she dies —
Nothing like a good funeral to get her juices going.
So: I'll stand as I stand. Duck. Tunnel. Horse. Chicken.
— Still, I love this tin-pot abecedarian song!
The last of the last hymns with the new cantor in hysterics,
Bellowing into the ceremonial factory light
Until, at last, we get up and get out of here.
I must shake the old Rebbe's hand. A son, my God! I mean it.

TO WIMAN FROM WALLA WALLA

— Washington

Dear Chris —

     On the road now I begin with the thing that hurts,
As some smarty says one must: There is a remedy for everything
Except death (though I think the French say that honey is not for asses).
It's been twelve hours of driving for two rounds of mimosas —
Let's call that our blood oath.
This morning the light at the outdoor breakfast was weak,
And even the potter's field, the acre of vineyards, and the new distillery
At Katrina's was a good thump reined in by spring light —
All of her syrupy kids in need of a bath by 8 A.M.!
That light over the morning had so much near-transparency in it,
Swerving and flicking and skimming against the heat rising on the hills.
And the wind was not so rowdy as it was a token of many ranges,
Not so much an ode to pleasure as an apologia for living,
As if the half-lost days —

               fervent days, shuttered days —
Can only be remembered in prayer
Where the blood unwrinkles like a shroud.
Once, miles from here on the coast in the Driftwood Library,

                             I overheard

A wounded woman read Auden to herself, out loud, but whispering,
Like a small child does who has just learned to read
With a slow, jaw-stretching, strung-along give and take
Between voice and mind, part panic, part rapture,
As if in her nervous system language was becoming unarrested.
We were in the Quiet Room with the magazines lined neatly
And the windows shined over with the flat light of the aqueous,
Wind-filtered air — sprouted light, stoked light, no more
Attached to *lament* than *head* is to *love*, than *human* is to *arm*.
She was whispering, "Lay your sleeping head, my love,

Human on my faithless arm . . ." over and over, as if the two lines
Were embryonic to a vanished burn or ache, as if the geology
Of *human* was mineral in the rock of *faithless.*

                                     Plenty makes us poor,
Says John Dryden, and despite what Saint Matthew says, even her reading
Can't heal the sick or cleanse the lepers, raise the dead or cast out demons.
Then the woman dropped off from the archways of words
Into a long moment of covenant, without pain or love,
Unbidden, moving inward, as into a gray valley of thought.
And as I watched her drifting to sleep in the quietness of the room,
I imagined for no reason that she was dreaming of a gardener's dog
That won't eat the lettuce but won't let others either.
I tell you this, Chris, with the confidence of an egg fighting a rock —
She was sleeping and Auden was the resin in her mind.
Earlier, on the drive home, over the high desert passes,
With the river arrested and pinned with new light,
Some logic sequined itself inside of me, a kind of inquest
I had to stomach, like the fear of dying. And even though it was spring
I was thinking of snowy ditches and endless flurries.

TO KELLER FROM SKAMANIA LODGE

— Stevenson, Washington

Dear Nick—

      The ospreys are nesting atop the telephone poles,
And six Canada geese just threaded over and missed the window
I'm looking through toward a mountain I gave up a marriage
On—though I haven't come here to recover so much as go on
To veer toward the false *veritas* of unmortal life.
Part citizen, part lapsed cognoscente, I stare at the late air
And imagine it's braided with judgment. The wind knifes
The sky, and the moon has yet to bumper over.
Did you really mean to say that thing about faith? Sometimes,
I know, faith is the Pearl Girl, sometimes Ming the Merciless.
                        Like: *Fides*, I want to say *Fides, fidere*.
But, Nick, all the Latin I've memorized has left me short of breath.
Consider this: When I look out now at this long field
I see that the shrubs, the flowers, the shade, and the liverish
Alienation that lacks the pleasure of indifference
Are no more cosmetic than they are a zeitgeist for the cosmos.
You were right to say prophets are brazen
And to believe that hope is the birth of songs.
But did you really mean to say, "'Yes' is a complete sentence," Nick?
Yes. I suppose you did. For me, it's fallible
And riddled as a ribbon of scarlet silk.
And, yes, Nick, I can hear lullabies of the lonely from another era.
—You would love this view! And, in the old days, this gin—
No matter. I can hear music rising now from one of the weddings
Started today in the high grass that has yet to be plowed in
And that trembles toward the river. At the end of the first wedding,
There's applause, a cello, and a revelation
That no one will understand for years.
At the end of the other wedding,

21

                         the cuddly party
Weaved through the tall grass like the revelers
Panting coldly in Keats' ode — with the lacy bride
Smiling into her yellow bouquet, and the young groom
Seeming to begin to breathe again.
                         I think you'd have loved
The uncertain crossroads,
The way the res publica made room
For the community
                  (it was like a window opening into a tattered wind).
Then the light got whippy and wrinkled and it hovered
Over the swallows that swept the sky down to the river's calm rings.
Faith is a verb you said. OK. We'll see.

TO RUEST FROM WINSTON-SALEM

— North Carolina

Dear Paul—

      From this banishment I can't see mothers or wise men—

Though the acres of engraved gardens in the lapsed tobacco plantation

Are a little balm and a little honey. And where children once rippled

In the lap of this big lawn—I mean in the ripped-out

Courtyard outside my window—there are now ghosts

Of dandelions to trace out the raw war and reverie.

Since we last talked—you heading to the Yucatan,

Me scratching my head over a tortured Thanksgiving

                        and the government

Collapsing like the last man in a family of pioneers—

There's been hardly anyone in this city to speak to.

Once, Paul, I was angry at danger—

                  and headed to Boston

Where my brethren couldn't find me.

They called for us to be reunited

                      but saw me as just a boy

Hidden in seedy woods and in windy alleys

And even in one uncut pasture where the sky tumbled.

True, that boy gave up hope that there would be any God

To deliver him into the divided arms of his people.

Then, once, lying in a grassy place

As if stretched out in a tub,

                he found cups of wind

To be his new brothers and heard them asking:

          Where have you gone, brother, how far

          Can a body travel and not die—tell us, brother,

          What is this life that sleeps like a dog near the fire?

For an hour now, Paul, I've been staring out the window,

                  whistling at the age.

Earlier I watched a white girl knit a tea towel,
And all I could think was to what should I turn
Now that I know words are not for love?
I thought: Everyone's mother is growing old,
And, like brush for the whitewash, she's biding her time —
Paul, I know too well that a man warned is half saved.
But if I could call the dawns and dusks to order
I'd call us all to the briny temple of light and dark
Where, astonishing in our robes, we'd be blushing and full-faced,
Full-blown, heraldic, and we'd have the rhythm
Of myrrh and high pangs,

                       and then, with a hokum-pokum,
We'd pray like mystics and not knuckle under.
And before long we'd hear the dead clamor
And we'd know that peace had come to their hearts.
Then the hair-sprayed ladies from the Sisterhood

                           would bring out the cookies!
Paul, those old tracks leading North now graze with grief.
Behind the windows of this Forsyth County
Station of rooms
Where I've landed with a plunk,
The mouths of the workmen

                   turn to mumbling.
And now I imagine virgins —

               Paul, you remember them,
They came to the last surprise party
You threw for yourself in Boston —
Even they have tumbled on gnarled thorns
As if caught in laughter, even they carry in their arms
Dry loaves of bread like sleeping infants.

                   I'm thinking of your North Shore mother
Blowing in and out of her white hospital room
As if check-marked by voices and waves.
You asked:

> *What of her dark richness*
> *and grievances and disappointments?*

Paul, I want to go on and say more about mothers,
But this hemmed-in mothy light limps into myth too easily
And the after-season lilacs preen too much
Like small girls sleeping on the grass.
And the gnats and the fleas and the flecking black flies
Shimmer and wheeze into the good night.
Now a violinist in the far courtyard
Sharpens the news into wishes
And the notes scurry like wrens from a fence.
All this I hum to you on a lazy autumn night,
As if stenciling in the dark.

TO GIFFORD FROM KIOWA COUNTY

—Oklahoma

Dear Giff—

    It's been so long since I've unwound,
And with the canyons here unrolling in red,
And the lake hustling up to the shattered stones
Like a lickerish wind on the hunt for comfort,
I've been thinking about the rain that pummeled last night,
Churning and crystal and prickly,
Whamming the sky with a whomping maw.
That sort of thunder could grind on—and it did—
Flashing the town into snow-globe vistas
Where the folk landscapes glisten
In the hopped-up, miniature, spoony light.
In the middle of that storm I wanted to say:
                            Blessed is the man
Who walks in the counsel of the ungodly,
And blessed the man who stands with sinners
And gentle believers.
Earlier, the morning wind flickered
                      in a bugle of twigs.
A labyrinth of light came on—
Then wandering in were these clouds,
Fleeting and grayish, frail, and shy.
It's the sort of weather that makes you hope
                  you get to Heaven
Half an hour before the devil knows you're there.
But I have not been meaning to write to you about the rain
                    or death or the debonair light.
There are moments here
When you can hear the snaky echoes
Rattle in the canyons like faint tufts of despair,

Unnamed and invisible,
That crackle with a faith
                  just as a white-tailed cloud passes.
You can hear the new century shuffling into war,
Where the strange cities submerge into toast and beer,
And the markets get spectacular with dark carts of apples
And fish and berries, leeks and cherries and currants,
And with the hawkers licking their tongues,
And the bidders as undiminished as days,
                        and all the while the stiff flags
Mutter above the flagstones with their homey dreams.
Surely, Giff, disillusion is the universal
                        consequence of war.
But I'm thinking it's the same with peace.
If the madmen take the courthouse,
If the pirates kidnap the blind girl,
If the composer refuses to indulge another note
Or the note he does indulge in
Spirals from the violinist's fingers
Like a streaming breath,
                  quizzical and dissolving,
Obvious and not at all dense,
Into the balconies of churches,
And the children join in with their waxy songs,
Ever louder,
            growing with the rhythm of weeping—
And even that note, like the eyes of the forgotten,
Rejects nothing—
Then I know that whatever nameless
Afterthought purifies
These knock-kneed words,
I still won't know anything
About the quartz in these canyons
Or the golden in this age.

It's friendship I'm speaking of,
Like the last poem of an epoch
That anyone can ever remember,
Into which the flowery dresses
Symbolize not truths but communion,
And the magpies sleep
                    like a slow wind
In the countries of dream.
Giff, I can see you now:
Striding across your Northampton lawns.
It's April, lilacs calm as the rivers,
The nighthawks not yet in bloom,
And the shadowy trunks of birches
Which have whitened at the end of winter
Harden now against oblivion.
On the town green, you're coming up to your beloved,
And you reenact, as rain does,
The flaws and sins and pleasures of this life,
Half-opened and amorous,
So that one's days of forgiveness
Are no different from one's days of penance.
And the air is darkening and cool
And timed to meet the devotional
                    flashes of light.
You are, it seems, happy.
Back here, in the landlocked
                    latitudes of my birth,
Where power still grows from the barrel of a gun —
                              I think Mao said that —
I fear I've gotten out of the mud and fallen into the river.
Outside now, clouds disappear
                    and the skies steal free.
Last night's rain unsurrounds the canyons,
And with everything on earth unready

28

And the creeds over-rejoiced,
And for reasons I don't understand
Not only fools need answers
And stay awake at night,

                   listening to storms,
But the oppressed still believe in mankind,
And the saintly among us grin at the sky,
I find myself longing for one living word
To last among a thousand dead ones —
Home — where the insignificant must be said
At this edge of our sun-squalled nation,
Among the slow waters and red rocks.

TO BIERDS FROM THE CANNERY PIER HOTEL

—*Astoria, Oregon*

Dear Linda—
    These Somali pirates could have burst
Like a black spot out of one of your poems if even one verse
Had a $9.99 inflatable raft in it. You read the news,
And what you think is: After William Kidd hung for weeks
At Tilbury Point—flared-up, rumpled, and fat-lipped—
Or Blackbeard on the HMS *Pearl* got beheaded—
This after his keelhauled runner, the *Queen Anne's Revenge*,
Went aground with a broken mast near Beaufort's Inlet—
Our cutthroats would have wished a lot less for fiddler's green.
But, hoisting their Jolly Roger, such good, grand gentlemen
Have yet to show themselves loaded to the gunwales
Or as much more than run-of-the-mill squiffies of the sweet trade.
Still: They have guns, go a-kidnapping, and earn more than the GDP.
Holidaying in this renovated cannery, Linda, I'm kept up
Nights by the blinking masts of steamers that slink
From the Pacific Ocean to the Columbia River
And back—lovely and reddened and silent.
                        You're miles north
On the island of Bainbridge, named for the same commodore
As the warship bearing down tonight on that wee pirate craft—
William Bainbridge, who plied his cat o' nine tails
In the Barbary Wars and later against the *Java* during the War of 1812—
And I imagine you studying up on pirate foods, embroideries, and laws,
From the Declaration of Paris to the Conventions of Geneva,
Because no poem has yet been made in the voice of Blackbeard's lass.
And while he paraded up and back o'er the Caribbean seas
With his swords and pistols and feathered tricorn,
She waited in a cathouse on the Isle of Man.
I want to see something of her came out of your visions,

33

                                              as if:

     She slumped in the corner of some night café,
     Her face, hair, the velvet choker at her throat,
     All cast in a yellowing limelight.

But our lass is just a poor, soft model saying your lines—
And this springtime estuary is not like wheat fields or corn silk hair.
Blackbeard's lass was no lily-livered girl either,
                                        lighting a candle
On the windowsill, staring west to fall into sleep
Past the time her man might have come home,
If a scurvy dog can be said to have a home.

                     She kept her diary like a womb,
Sketching babies and peonies and fairies, wrote:

     God spoke to me last night like an accident. A furious
     Unhappiness took my mind as God had bred it into my dreams.
     Such death I did not want, such denials and injustice and darksome
     Disputations—all revealed to my heart like a dull fire.
     I did not want that, but the textures of my words were sophistries.
     I scrawl this for you, my long lost one, my soul, my mate.

                        —I know
Some of that feeling, Linda, having moved and moved,
City to city, from here to thar' and with all me hearties left behind
Or, lately, turning away from their certain selves. Bloody pirates!
But: To head toward sea, dilated and shingled, trashed as a heart,
And then setting sail to suffer and show how manly we are
Working the slip rings on, packing the over-unders,
Deferential as empty thrones, neatly gathering up our black snakes
To depart for atonement, that's the life for makers of poems—
Forsaken, melodramatic, and sack-clothed.

                   And the restlessness we might plunder,
And the distracted meditations that lead us, bothersomely, landward
With our absorption and frailty and voices spinning over
Into darkness in the alien rooms—these are the crimes we sob out
With flushed cheeks, chastened and breathless,

34

Ablaze with inspiration and fortune and injustice,
Mythologizing, line by knotty line,

                              until...Ahoy! and Avast!
This private life is no longer a tale of bondage, wind, and fright.

TO ANSEL FROM THE HOTEL ANDRA

— Seattle

Dear Talvikki —

    For days I've been thinking about this verse:
Stand in awe and sin not, commune with your own heart.
From somewhere early in Psalms, but I'm not
Having much luck with either the *commune* part or the *awe* —
Sinning I've mastered with a lead foot.
What I mean is, human reason is lovely and courageous.
Just now, as the protesters on 4th Avenue
Drew the city out to the balconies above the rainless gray,
Shouting, "War criminals! War criminals!"
I thought of the posture you've taken
To live as silently as an unfurled sail.
In the demonstration, about a dozen anti-war-criminal types
In crappy T-shirts were kangaroo-kicking

                    for the tour-bus pilgrims,
Passing in front of the Dahlia Bakery
Where once, over the sweetest apricot jam,
I swore to give up loneliness and study the dicey
Fissure between *flibbertigibbet* and *boilerplate*.

              What I figured was:
Both establish the ideas of words and thought,
Both guide us to insist on truth and the ideal —
Even if we scribble oppression into our hearts —
And both are the plenary for austere and tortured souls.
But, Talvi, this sort of talk is just Pooh-Bah-ism.

                    Forgive me.
It was in Amherst, Talvi, at Emily Dickinson's house
That we last talked about this sort of blufferage.
We were standing in her backyard in an inch of late
Spring snow, coatless because of the quickening sun,

In straw-colored light and a prickly wind, on a Sunday,
With the house locked, and us in the empty back lot.
If ever a woman survived by the motto, "Live
So you won't be ashamed to sell the family parrot
To the town gossip," it was Emily Dickinson.
How I wanted just to finger the blue ribbons
She took for the bake-offs at the town fair.

                                        Oh, my county hen!
I can see her with us in that blooming morning,
You and I like nihilists who spiral into our epoch with a kerplunk,
Or like heretics who know seeing is done with one's own eyes.
And, from this hotel-window balcony, what I see
Are the purring backhanders, out-of-towners, and vagrants,
And suddenly I understand that this window
I could leap from — if I were given to desperate impulse —
Might as well be the window to my old life,
Clear and so full of clarity, like a wronged man, it's become.
All my former gardens and patios, pots, beds, and mail posts,
Lampshades and rickety switches,
The highboy and the tarnished silver,
The armchairs and frayed rugs and book-lined walls
Have come into view here like 10,000 afterthoughts,
As if a heart is made of these and not misery,
As if the fingers I have touched in love or in grief,
In witness or in betrayal,
Could've been touched by my hand a century ago
Or even yesterday —
So that time is a canal to sail a small boat through
With the blue sails snapped sharp.
Such letters, my dear, leave us too separated —
A hand, a breeze, a little sun in the back of memory.
It's raining solitude now — pearling the city —
As if this letter were written by clouds.

TO DI PIERO FROM DUFUR

— Wasco County, Oregon

Dear Simone —

      I've descended toward the county line

Of a haunted mood, and I am ashamed

To have forgotten so many customs,

As you said I might that night in San Francisco

When the scrub jays in the window

Clapped like incantations and barbarian prayers,

Clapped and poured glory

Onto a dozen universal ideas

                that have traveled

From Podunk to capital city and back.

Like this by-passable, high desert, grassy town, too,

With its post-pioneer turn-of-the-century hotel

Giving us rooms for the night.

            In 1907

The town pharmacist built this brick boardinghouse,

Forty-five years after the village held its first church meeting.

The mail didn't make it until fifteen years later,

Though the kids from one generation to the next,

Like spores from a wildflower,

            have moved on

With their knowledge of flatbread and boredom —

And with the town mothers left behind to whistle at blackbirds

And with the town fathers left, too, without pity from God —

Though all the children believe they can return

As if returning from a far field before dark

To speak the language of a sketched-out wind.

Meanwhile, right now, this breeze

And the first wrathless days of high desert sunlight

Rustle with thorny recitations of spring —

There are clouds gathering, Simone, and it looks bad.
So now, with a cold draft sweeping in
From the opened window across my bare arms
Like an inherited forgotten prayer of mist,
I realize I have held out a chair to death
                              long enough,
Even if the years still only half-open and shiver
And the mind seeks kinship
                    with the ecstasies of light.
I was going to tell you, however,
About the mountain in the distance.
It's visible from the second-storey balcony,
                    right *there,*
And hovers in the west as the West,
As if painted onto the sky,
Snowy in the cloudless air
                        like a white scent
Or the impeccable divination of the everyday
With its streams burbling underground
And its bare places facing the sun
With flowerless promises of midsummer.
Or—let me tell you about what's beyond that,
                        cutting in and out of the skies:
The flight paths of a dozen gulls
Careering over the truss bridge of Astoria
                    181 miles from here—
Gulls like mystics that dissolve
Above the gray-spattered waves.
These are the gulls of exultation and gulls of retreat,
Gulls of the lost chances to bloom in springtime and be saved
And gulls of communion and martyrs and forbidden places,
And gulls of Jews who abandoned the saints.
These gulls cry, Simone, for the sacraments
Of lingering vigils and ruddy joys.

And they hover, however clipped, in the upper white
Wind-whipped wounds of the sky,
Hover and ache with their stained wings,
Hover where the river salts into the sea.
If you were here, I'd call you confessor to these gulls —
You, the bruiser, the cuddler,
Content with getting on past a late vision,
A little rasping, and a sharp-toothed swear.
I wish, today, I could call you that.
— But it's just the rattling gulls,
Humping and jiving and loose —
Then, suddenly, like a song for order and calm,
Having cried out toward an endless nothing,
They go lyre-backed and quiet
                              like easy hours.
And now, out of the mountain comes the rain,
Rippling in the curves and pivots and tumult
                              of this harbor
Of hills, humping against this hotel —
Rain and more rain and dirty rain,
More rain than even a poor farmer could hope for,
Apparitional and panoramic rain, foretelling
And flashing and implicit rain,
                              the unspent story of rain,
A rip-toothed American West of rain,
A magnum opus of rain, a jig of a good man's
                              political liberty of rain,
Rain with the music of brutish trains I heard in dreams,
And the potbellies I carried up and down stairs,
And the invisible flame of God I couldn't find.
Rain that's idiomatic and immaculate, that condenses
The hours into parcels of sleepless years,
Wringing out the myth of one past,
Wringing out the myth of another past

The way the bodies of lovers get wrung out
                    in the hours of flame and dark.
Simone, I'm trying to remember
All the good friends in the rush of the world,
And I'm not sure anymore what road I've traveled.
From here on out, I swear to nod at old men
And greet the sun with less fright.
I know that when the rains clear
                    and night petals the valley
And sinks into a quilt of mist,
The white clouds will stumble to the ground,
And the last of the light will slip off into the low grass,
And that will be the next tongue to speak.

TO FARNSWORTH FROM BAR AVIGNON

— Portland

Dear Bob —

      Some mornings a man is so aroused in his naked sleep
He's more assassin than sire, rotting in the cloister
Of what his heart was before the summer makes his days.
He thinks: *He that dreams the world slays the wicked.*
But I wonder if learning to die is any simpler
Than listening to the nearby trains clanging.

                     Tonight, marigold-warm
With a breezy light, nearest to happy as I've known

                          and buoyant
As a tramp doing his trampiest dance among sparrows,
I sit outside at this sidewalk table on Division Street
With my gin and tonic beside a table of three American women
Talking French in preparation for a trip to Paris.
Three beautiful, American, French-speaking women!
Not that they were speaking to me, I mean —
I'm waiting for my great love to arrive,

                 and she will, sudden
As the floor of a valley opening all at once
To flowers and smoke and the early chirrup of evening.
Waiting, I begin to remember the time I found that little forest on fire
In Ringer Park in Boston —

             Jeff Smith started it and denies it still! —
I'd come upon the flames walking Tut the dog into the woods.
It was a sad fire, a disquieted fire, but not devastating,
A kind of after-Paradise-low-wheeze-in-the-spring-grass of a fire
That Tut pawed at with his milky paw.
— How enduring memory is, Bob, in a decent pub. —

             Another time, at the Zoo Bar
Outside the Freud Hilton in Washington, D.C.,

We came around to talk of bugging out of the capital
          and both of us turning
To the quaint, square-laden villages of New England —
As if we believed we could swear away
The point that love knows no law.
Besides, what faith in virtue was needed for that?
Bob, the French-speaking women
          are now happily chatting
With their chardonnay,
          with their miniature dictionaries for coasters,
With the beginning of their travels still ahead of them
Like a small tree on the horizon —
Three women between aging and old,
Between, I think, one man and the next.
                    I want to tell you, Bob,
                    urgency is imperfect —
Like pulling a coat to the chin in the style of an immigrant,
Donnish and idle and landed,
Lamenting and fasting and unrocked by consent,
An immigrant who knows that it's best to dream away
The affairs of bloody men and women —
                    my old drunken ways, Bob!
Ah, now this street, too, is oafish and sweet,
And the barkeeps are the faces of my home.
          Bob, I tell you, I have faced rivers,
Been to the world's end,
Been without end to where I could not attain the Earth.
So I know this: Only once has a great fire
Led me to know my own heart — after first dismantling it
And calling morning, evening, and calling hate, love.
I wish the night body were less sweet, less dangerous.
Mornings, it's ashamed and confessional,
Undressed, sumptuous, ugly, miraculous,
Stirring out of its vaporous silences.

I'm not talking about:
Some comprehension of good and evil, Bob,
Nor anything like a child in search of a mother,
Nor of a father's unpracticed wince at the unlearning of time.
I'm not much talking about the terror of love, either,
But something like it where the ally of being is the body
And, where beauty exists, it's a fire blazing
Like the chirrups of red birds and the sprawling
Masquerades and invocations of flowery things:
A tablet for writing, a compass,
       a scroll, a lyre,
An aulos, a veil,
A tragic mask, and a comic mask.
          — So now I think of you
Sailing the late waters off the coast of Maine
In Sunrise County
       with the night cafés gone dead.
The waves heave in drifts, unhistorically so,
And have the color of weather or marble.
You have the till, yes? With one eye unshut
Against the brine of the waters off the bay?
With your quiet pastures and secrets?
As if you could stare into an upside down mirror of time?
This, then, for those who have suffered much,
Who will awaken in the unhappened future
In which all that might be misunderstood
Is at last comprehended,
In which giving one's life to a single task
Is to know that it may never get accomplished.

TO COLLIER FROM UNITED FLIGHT 304

—Austin to Greensboro

Dear Michael—

        These skies redden

With the clowniest of fat clouds

And sway between elation and sadness

Before turning a more deeper red

Deeper across Tennessee and Mississippi.

The clouds sway against the barriers of time

And grandmas and gurgling infants,

And all the strangers jammed in here

Indifferent to subterfuge or tears

Thirty-five thousand miles

        above the buried

Bodies of the old Confederacy,

Where the very young,

Amazed by their wounds,

Understand only a little

Of how their vast emotions wing

From spring to summer

Like unnamed devilish gifts

Or spurs in the valley,

A rocky river bend,

These gold-and-yellowing trees—

Down there, even the young

Can't make out this plane

        through the poorly hung clouds,

Inside which I imagine

All love breathes

With a sudden snort and a leg-jerk

As evening comes.

Up here, if you were to ask

If I believed in free will
I'd have to say, *I have no choice,*
And lean my head harder
Against the small window
Like an unimportant child
Staring at his own consciousness.
Tomorrow, little of this twilit view
Will stay with me—
The kidney-shaped pools
And undarkened starlings,
The schoolyards and ball fields,
The unincorporated spidery roads
And the lonesome houses
Atop the farms and their stubbly miles.
But even as the mist rises and falls
Across the horizon, and the sun,
Like a silent hymn for the wronged,
Passes from red to black
To invisible as if surviving time,
I will lean my head back
And dwell on the sloping vision
Of my wax-paper bride,
Who waits for me with a nest for a ring
And prayers in her heart
Under a low sky of lightning bugs,
Where there are no lullabies.
She vibrates in the terra firma of home.
—I hope you're not offended
By such sentimental muttering.
—Twelve nights ago
                    your toast to Stan
Was like strolling through a pleasant garden
Where there occurs a certain kind
Of unconcerned transformation

That might be called love in another age,
When men—and I mean, men—
Spoke openly about the precisions of joy
And the precisions of pain
So that both obliterate their usual blurriness,
The differences between blessed
And treasure and wonder
Not so different from those
Between throb and gnaw and burn.
                    Michael, it's autumn again,
More so than I expected.
These days I don't want to be the skeptic
Who, even when he sees the handwriting
On the wall, winces
As if certain it's a forgery.
I mean, to the question
Is the glass half full or half empty
I want to say, c'mon, man,
The glass is twice as tall
As it needs to be.
                    There are days now that I wonder
Where and under what wind at night
Have you taken refuge in your history of solitude,
Long swims, and empty trains,
And whether your ironic smiling,
Smart as the dog-eared
How to Keep Your Volkswagen Alive
                    manual you keep on hold,
Can match the way you handle
So much shadow and blood
As if handling every situation
One might come across with any air-cooled Beetle
Built through 1978
That rumbles on America's circuitous roads

Like those down there—
Somewhere below, right now, it's Nashville,
Michael, and the pool I trained at in 1985,
When I did not know you,
Or your sister who dived
In the '64 Games in Tokyo—
That year the hardest dive I learned
From the ten-meter platform
Was a back one-and-one-half
With three-and-a-half twists—
And, a lot of the time, the overly
Soft way I started the trick
With my head tipped a little too far down
Left me splayed when I got to the water,
Legs entwined, mad-capped,
Like a corkscrew bent in two.
Other times, I'd square it up,
And from a few meters
Above the surface of the water,
When you're falling gnarly
And fast like that,
You can get a good look at your entry spot
With all that smooth blue surface to pierce into
(Before finally) ripping it
With a spittle of splash
No bigger than a teardrop.
The body, when it falls
Out of the sky like that,
Opens and spills,
Spirals and unwinds,
Like a daffy angel
Delivered from danger—
Not that I have much interest in fallen angels.
But like an angel, nonetheless,

Michael, delivered from death.
And yet: Falling is not like dying
Or even forgetting the dead,
But remembering the living
In a spin of reconciliation,
Like *past* changing its name to *future*,
Winter becoming *summer*.
The dive complete,
The surface flat again.
The diver holding his breath
               under the warm water.
Michael, I like it up here
In this sky tonight,
Even with all the thighs and elbows
Going stiff, the broad stewardess
Flirting with business class,
A whiff of *mercy*
And the *end of days*
And *rest in peace*
All wrapped into our descent,
Fine as grace, fine as true love,
Even faith, and a hope now
That the wings will level
And some of the evil
The world has suffered
Will rumple into a mild fall.
           I hope death is like that, don't you?
Put down with ease,
A kind of testament
To training and luck,
So that the heaviness
Is not unendurable but endured.
Is this what it means
To feel compassion for others,

Unfolding in the flesh
Where all the descendants
Of human tenderness
Unmake the same world,
                    landing at last
Along the track lights, and fulfilled?
— You're a thousand miles from here
In a Green Mountains evening
In far-gone Vermont,
Where handfuls of patriots died so long ago,
The Founding Fathers we decipher to death,
Who built houses and bent rivers,
Who formed schools and furrowed farms,
And then turned graves into cities
Where they cut sorrow out of stone,
And where they sweat bliss
And rubble and new hope.
— Holy, holy, holy, Michael!
We're out of the sky,
And back on earth.

TO BUCKLEY FROM BERKELEY

—California

Dear Bill—

      Maybe you'd like the first hundred names
From the New York City phone book to run the government,
But I'd prefer the names came from out here in the West
Among the bare-assed and tan and with a bitchin' view of the Bay
So they can remember that even the most criminal or golden heart,
Islanded behind a thought,
Must never forget that the tides come to the rocks
And not the other way around,
That when a notion is lit, like these foghorn waters
Sprinkled by car-lights and bridge-lights are lit,
A notion becomes lust for thieves
And nutty professors and sock-in-the-ear,
Disputatious, child-minded pundits—
The spitters and brainiacs and dekes each foresworn to the ideal
That, sad as it is to say, they've become those people
Who would enormously be improved by death,
Or else spun loose with wanderlust
And a premium sense of their own lap-doggy selves.

                       That, Bill, and also this:
The tides here, drifting at the end of the Pacific's ebb,
Whooping against the rocks on the harbor,
Are not only washout and whitecap,
                 devour and pain,
But they also form, in my mind, a goofy consciousness
That if it is better to trust the Lord
Than to put confidence in man,
Then I am sincerely worried about both,
And that as I watch the sun set,
As I while away the tide-breaks,
I imagine an occasion where, inland,

You and I might stroll into a shabby cornfield
And dream of looking westward, then east,
And then, together,
We would wave at the landlocked gulls
And unheard-of foam
And notice and admire the gargantuan stalks
That swim up to the Midwestern stars —
Stalks that, with the wind, growl against idea and ideal,
So that, as the Chinese say,

                     when you bow, Bill, bow low,
And if not that, then they growl in favor of the idea and ideal
That a fat insurance man from Hartford says
Means the sea is a genius,
That it forms neither a mind nor a voice,
That it flutters and mimics and cries
And is completely inhuman,

                     or else incompletely,
And therefore something we ought not mask
As we mask all manner of love,
As we winnow away our imbroglios,
As we canoodle with nudnicks,
As we make songs and dances,
Or as we crow about turning the tide from your ideas to mine,
Or from thinking to feeling,

                     conservation to expressiveness,
And on and on, from rain to sun,
And then even more turning,
Until we swear only to swear —
That, Bill, is not seriousness,
That is a mollycoddled, gussied-up shakedown.
But this bay, Bill, contains a message for America, too,

                     and it is this:
That the waters slam against the rocks,
But the rocks are unconvinced,

That the red drifting in the new clouds
On the horizon is good,
That the small boats with fathers and uncles
Heading out and laying down their nets
Have not brought guns or dogs,
Testaments or declarations.
But these men of the shore
Have brought their hunger
As they fished under the California light,
Fished, as now, into dusk,
Fished against the cold quick currents,
Against the shining scales of the day
With the slack lines dropped
Below where the sunlight frees itself into the shadows.
And so they fished against notions
                              like *freedom*, like *determination*—
Until all of that handsome chatter sinks
And vanishes under the shoals,
Sinks and vanishes like dull enchantments
Among the lichen and the sea flowers,
Among the dilated shipwrecks and the quiet mussels—
So that now, Bill, when I think of you
                              in the Heaven of Purest Thought,
My mind goes velvet with the cruel quarrels,
Goes undertowed and undersea,
From weariness with MacGuffins and Cubists and Plebes,
Until all that is left is a dance hall of sweethearts,
And where even the mere unsung among us,
Ribbed with sea-shine, rise to sight
In the heaves and breaks and slick tingles of the Bay,
And where a hundred of this city's collectivists
Are reading up on the Constitution
And finding it not so bad, really,
Not so bad, Bill, not really.

TO CONDA FROM ANACONDA

—Montana

Dear Cesar—
            Just off the highway
From here is Opportunity.
The town's not living up to its name.
And no one's singing *O tempora! O mores!*
Not since the copper company
Gave everyone a day's notice
Twenty-nine years ago next September.
What's left is the smelter stack
That bricks up 585 feet closer-to-God high
Like an unfaithful steeple.
Even the stained glass
Inside the lovely St. Mark's on Third Street
Honors the radial heights in its east windows.
From the highway, what you see
Is a sun-rusted mausoleum to 1919 masonry—
So tall and wide you can slip
The Washington Monument into it.
                              Say, Cesar, can you see
The Anaconda stack from your porch in old Virginia?
Or the rusty gas that spewed for 61 years
Across the hard land that accepts nothing?
There were 4 million cubic feet of gas per minute,
I don't know how you could have missed it.
Like most tragedies in America,
It's a state park now.
As for the town, it got splayed
In half and hasn't got up yet.
All big government did was try to clean up
The miles after miles of slag heap

Along the dark road into here,
Slag still black with the souls
Sold to the company store,
Where what you get
Is another year older
          and deeper in debt.
There are 30 bars in this town, Cesar,
And 60 percent of the folks are over 65.
Eight miles from the Continental Divide,
The median income is $26K.
Lucille Ball lived here and so did Frank Cope,
Starting tackle for the N.Y. Giants 1938–1947.
                              This morning
Outside the Locker Room Bar
I met one old-timer with good hair
Who used a dollar to buy potatoes
To boil for dinner with salt and butter.
He told me about walking to the edge of Anaconda
When he turned 24
Twenty-nine years ago next September,
Not far from where the back country squawks
At the night and the moon gathers
Over the mocking birds and company-built houses
Crammed onto the tree-named streets —
Oak, Pin, Chestnut, Locust, Beech, Cedar, Cherry.
They come at you like a song,
Like *America the Beautiful,*
Like *'Taint Nobody's Business If I Do.*
Cypress, Dogwood, Cottonwood, Elm —
And he told me he dreamed of leaving Anaconda
For Butte, where the political lords
Know how to shake the state for jobs,
Or else leave for Opportunity
Or West Valley or Phillipsburg

Where the degrees of gray
Blow into an utterance
Only a harpy can translate,
A squall, like some unknown language
That sounds like dirt mixed with dust.
Suddenly, there's another man
Across Commercial Street
Talking openly about impotence —
Then about death and birth
And sorrow and gases and death
And rare clear nights from some other year
When the kids who have abandoned this town
                              used to get a dollar
At the Smelterman's Day Picnic in July
And got to ride a pony for free
And later watch Legion ball in Washoe Park,
And where no one ever wanted to believe
In sorrow because it seemed anti-American.
Cesar, that old man stood on Commercial Street
Half in shadow, half in sweat, and half in fear
That fit him like a flannel shirt from 1974,
The year India got the bomb
And called it *Smiling Buddha*,
When in Troy, Ohio, the first UPC code
Was used to sell a pack of Wrigley's gum,
When Haile Selassie was deposed
As was George Foreman by Ali in Kinshasa,
When Derek Jeter was born
And Duke Ellington died,
And when Nixon threw in the towel.
                      That was
Outside the Locker Room Bar.
Inside, it was 9 A.M., and the owner,
Joey Stranieri, aged 70 on tiptoe,

With the blue eyes of the old country
Around about near Napoli,
And a disease in his blood
So rare no one can name it,
Turned out to be the father
Of my brother-in-law
That works with cons
Two states away.
Joey poured us hot cups of coffee
And talked about his 26 years
Teaching biology at the Junior High.
      Cesar, I want you to look closely
At the National Guard poster
Side by side with the World Beer Cup poster,
The video poker and the Keno
And the black-and-white 8 × 10s
Of Anaconda High's great stars
From 60 years ago
Including 1956 U.S. Olympic boxer Johnny Rouse—
1956, the year Elvis made it
With "Heartbreak Hotel,"
My Fair Lady opened in New York,
"Under God" was added to the Pledge of Allegiance,
"In God We Trust" became the national motto,
Martin and Lewis called it quits,
As did the Montgomery bus boycott.
Cesar, here's a 1980 menu from the Copper Club,
Closed Mondays, and then forever:
Rib Steak, $4.25,
Australian Lobster Tail, $8.50,
Ravioli for the Italians
Who immigrated here for crummy jobs
That let them raise a family on smelt copper,
Including Joey's old man from the Mezzogiorno

Who died when the boy was in the third grade,
                                a la carte, for $2.25.
"Junior High's condemned now," says Joey,
Pouring in a little more joe.
                        That's when my mind closes
Around its dead gymnasium,
Closes around the gates chained
To the top of the slag hills
And the small pocket park
That does not exist in the center of town
Because the State of Montana
Wouldn't give the permit—
But if you want to plant
A kitchen garden in your backyard
And grow tomatoes and green beans
The State of Montana doesn't require a permit—
My mind still closing around the barbed fencing
Meant to keep gawkers off the slag hill.
All of it now is like three cheers
For the hours of corrosion
And inertia and semi-success,
For the foundry makers
And the half-gassed vegetables
And the raspy eulogies on eternity
And the idle hands
And the snow on the mountainsides
I looked at with curiosity while standing
Outside the Locker Room Bar
Before getting into my rented Chevy
To drive to Bozeman. —
Cesar, two nights ago in Missoula
At Pearl's Bar on Higgins Street
I ate elk for the first time.
I don't recommend it.

Stick with the Caesar salad.
But after Anaconda I was heading to Bozeman,
February snow chasing me from the west,
Sunlight in the east breaking through the clouds
Whining into the sky
With all the dust I've swallowed all these years.
On I-90, I saw two bald eagles
On two bald trees,
And I can't say I felt unhappy,
But I can't say I felt rich either.
   — I was thinking, Cesar,
Someone should write a *tanaga*
About the towns of Montana
In Tagalog, a language I love but cannot speak,
As my Anaconda friend cannot speak
The language of hope or change:

   Oh, be resilient you men
   And ladies. Anaconda
   Won't come back. Do not cower.
   The marketplace will save you.

I didn't see any Filipinos in Anaconda.
But I did see an Italian named Joey Stranieri
Whose mother came to America from Tuscany
And who drove me across town in his red Jeep
Even though we'd never met,
But he'd just learned
That his son's wife is my wife's sister.
In Montana, that's family.
In Montana, there are three fundamental principles
Given to the citizens: the right to due process of law,
The right to equal protection, and number three,
There's a guy in Butte what needs a job.
    At Mount Olivet
The Catholics are buried

And rest atop the best view of the valley
And the town and the smelter smokestack
That no longer belches
Across the big airy
But sits like a high school trophy
Behind the glass case inside the Locker Room Bar
Where, from time to time, the dudes stop
Before they head home to houses
Where blossoms have fallen to nothing,
So to admire what the young people
Don't stay long enough to notice,
The future slick and smiling
In a stiff-armed running back's face from 1948 —
A year in which Mahatma Gandhi fasts in Dehli
And is killed eighteen days later,
In which the Hell's Angels started in California
And the Marshall Plan started in France,
In which Israel was founded
And racial segregation ended in the Army,
In which Baryshnikov was born
And Babe Ruth died.
        Cesar, I have no idea
How to worship at the steeple in Anaconda —
To be cynical or devout,
To sing a miner's song
Or just breathe the airless air.
All this living without, all these years.
That's America, too,
Eight miles from the Continental Divide
Where no one leaves for work
And everyone returns to bed,
And not God or animal, man or child
Knows what to do about it.
What would you do with your theories

Composed by Jack Kemp,
Who grew up among Jews
In the Wilshire section of Los Angeles,
Quarterbacked for the Buffalo Bills 1962–1969,
Who believed that wounded towns
Like this could come back
If they just wait long enough,
Stay patient, preserve the old buildings
In zones of desire,
What with good back-country hiking nearby,
Or the right company to come along
And get the money circulating?

> *Whatever's here remains here.*
> *It's nowhere else and nothing.*
> *Its name is Anaconda.*
> *Dirt, slag, and easy temper.*

In the three hours I spent in Anaconda
I saw the earth eating the fence posts.
I saw the ferocity of repose.
I saw one bowling alley
And one Veterans of Foreign Wars Hall,
And a guy named Dan who said,
"Take it easy, Dave," at noon
When I left the Locker Room Bar,
As if I might came back later in the day,
Same as the copper.
But I did not see you, Cesar Conda,
I saw only what the children will inherit.
I did not see you
Among the opened bellies
And the hidden bones,
Among the candor and rage and sudden
Red mountain flowers
Near where the rivers burn

And the stones are crushed
And the shadows unflatten
From the wreckage of ground
In a mad dance.
No, I did not see you.
I did not see you.
Cesar Conda, come to Anaconda.
Come to Anaconda, Cesar Conda.

TO WENDY FROM THE GERSHWIN HOTEL

—New York City

My dear—
       Have I told you yet about my dream of the couple
That stood with gladness under the old grapevine
And who put silver pegs into the ground to find the sages
They called *moon* and *stars,* called *enemy* and *avenger*?
And when they were done standing awhile,
The light of that fussed-over late afternoon
Dissolved over them, the light
Like a warm meadow in springtime.
If they could have made themselves into one being
Like a statuette made of salt,
They'd have become a single saint in a dusky garden
Who suddenly was not so certain about his vow of poverty
And who knows no one alive
Can turn a thousand probabilities into one truth.
But, then, there was the other dream,
Later at night in this hotel
In which I can barely sleep
With the winter city blowy as tattered tinsel,
A dream I had of fearing robbers
Who were after our hearts
And who said strange things full of warning:
       Beware a small leak.
       Beware the fury of a patient man.
       Beware false knowledge.
       Beware the barrenness of a busy life.
       Beware a door with too many keys.
It took a curt nimbleness to awake from those dreams—
I mean, to come upon that couple in the damp night
Was to find they had grown to love old wool

And olives, and also wine, and sat out in the fading light
To drink and listen for the trees to grow still.

My dear,

I've spent too many hours in this city—
Somewhat starving, often naked, hardly hysterical,
With the nights vaudevillian as an old ache.
Once, you said, you dreamed a new motto for yourself:
Moot the trouble that becomes a loss.
I said: *Moot the worn-out unease.*
Or did I dream that? Or was it only a thought
Such as: *Are these new leaves or old ones*
On the mottled trees in the city Walt Whitman

calls Manhatta?

Moot the candled colors on the walls at night.
Moot the lies we have dipped into each other's hearts, and feared.

Earlier tonight, my dear,

I sang licks from "Summertime"
With Paul Ruest at the Ace Hotel on West 29th Street.
We drank whiskey for many hours—
With Paul, living is always easy!
The fish are jumping! And the cotton is high!
We drank whiskey and talked about old lives—
I will tell you, my dear, he misses his mother.
Come closing, he asked a lovely office worker in a tight dress
About her sparkly yellow drink, and she called it

Hop Skip and Go Naked #2.

Once in Venice at Harry's Bar I drank a Bellini #2—
That's raspberry not peach.
In fact I drank four of them and stumbled
Into the cobbled *sera*
And tipped my hat and dawdled by carts with trinkets
As if my body had become pure benediction,
And where, in that grainy air,
To exist as one who is confused and a little sour

Suddenly ceased inside me for a moment,
Where in my heart
>   *lamentation* became *hymn,*
>   *curse* became *wonder,*
>   *pain, abundance.*
>   And then, *gratitude.*

My dear, I stumbled into the Venetian light,
And the water, everywhere you looked, was furrowing.
I didn't see a single saint
>   but the pigeons

Wheeled and folded and had a saintly coo.
Whatever their beliefs are, was a mystery to me
And to the dethroned skies
And to whatever Vivaldian angels turned to shadows.
Here, at the Gershwin Hotel, night, too, is furrowing —
>   you are miles westward where the fig trees

Have begun to unravel, and the alley behind the house
Flashes like a small stream,
Flashes like a parable of blooming,
Like the bright art of silence
Replenished and otherworldly —
The days lifted out of the languorous vision
As if out of this bursting city
That has no time to beg
And no time to nurture eternity.
>   *I could cry salty tears,*
>   *Where have I been all these years?*
>   *Little wow, tell me now,*
>   *How long has this been going on?*

I hum it into the morning at the Gershwin Hotel.
I hum it and do a little dance,
Hopping up and down alone
In this small room,
A jig on one foot, a trot on the other,

Waving my arms in the naked hour
As the sun glazes over the East River,
A little woebegone,
A little like an instrument for the world.

> *Kiss me twice, then once more.*
> *That makes thrice. Let's make it four!*
> *What a break, for Heaven's sake!*
> *How long has this been going on?*

It's been going on, my dear, it's been going on,
And some days, it's the one and only grace
Half hidden, for sure, in a slippery dream.

TO SMITH FROM NORTHAMPTON

—Massachusetts

Dear Jeff—
      God knows why the Jews of the twentieth century
Put their Yiddish Book Center in the center of Jonathan Edwards'
Protestant Western Mass. Luke and I found it
                    on St. Joseph's Day
On the way to Emily Dickinson's (closed for the season).
So: From outside her windows, again,
                I imagined a small hand
Writing the words *spider* and *light*, *despair* and *heft*.
And that was about all I got from the place.
Plus the exceptional hedges.
—Jeff, it's late winter, hard rain, harder wind,
And the Oxbow River flooded
Above the trunks of trees,
The Oxbow grumbling at spring.
In Western Mass., about half an hour from Giff's house on Harlow Street,
The wind is never a gift, and the children, therefore,
                    are dropping
Their store-bought flowers and turning away
From the Oh, Come On! Spring Festival.
Just outside of town, driving now for hours in and out of rain
And the threat of rain,
I suck on my little ditch of afterthoughts—
They straggle without hubbub.
Who's a victor in this part of the world, I want to ask?
What with the narrow roads and clapboard houses
And dainty-apron'd matrons—
And the roads all ruddy and far from the honky-tonks
I grew up around in Harris County, Texas,
Where the women are divided by height and class,

69

And the men grow as quiet as stars.

And, strange as it may be,

That's when I think of the last Western sandwich

I ate in one of those greasy spoons on NASA Road 1,

Three and a half decades ago.

I can still taste the melted butter burnt in the skillet!

And the minced onions

And the eggs and the chopped ham,

Dash of pepper, slices of toast

                        that were so thin

They tasted like quiet disbelief.

The eggs so soft and well-fried, Jeff!

It was like the pleasure of God keeping me out of hell.

                                I remember, too,

A wren, suddenly, in the threshold of the diner's door —

It was a cactus wren,

                    a healer, solitary.

You'd think no one would turn against it in that back-road diner

With its feed bag décor.

But that wren tried to tear through a window,

And the glass and the bird lay at our feet —

I want to say it was like a prattle of empty-handed fears

But it just lay there.

And all the gentleman's gentlemen of the joint

Did absolutely nothing.

One dude, near whose feet

                the wren had died,

Spied at me like a cobra.

In the moment of understanding between us,

I knew my life was not worth hocking to get worked up about it.

That was then. That was Texas.

                    In Western Mass.,

In the season of Lent with the rivers flooded,

Days before your son's to be born

into the unpaged century,

I begin to remember, as if in a dream,

A hundred Yiddish sayings good for a boy like yours:

A man cannot jump over his own shadow.

A dog without teeth will also attack a bone.

A bad peace is better than a good war.

If you don't want to do something, one excuse is as good as another.

A man comes from dust and in the dust he will end—

And in the meantime it is good to sip a little gin.

The names of sons, Jeff, are like the number of days.

True, the old days are easier and easier to remember—

When the worry we had most wasn't fathers

but scoring a good spliff.

Ergo love. Ergo all of half of what was at hand.

As even now, steering into the Pioneer Valley of Hampshire County,

Into a town in which no one is grieving over the reichsmark

Or the end of Calvin Coolidge's mayorality,

I imagine Giff is standing in the center of his map room

right about now,

Studying the back roads in red between Hadley and Belchertown,

Considering the landmarks

like the Bridge of Flowers and Mt. Tom

And the homestead, west of Cummington, of William Cullen Bryant.

And, Jeff, of course, you know my companion

Has been present all this time—

my 17-year-old boy,

Dozing in the passenger seat like a good lad.

He sleeps with a little trouble and a little calm.

I know, times like this,

I'm trawling toward the next horizon and facing the evening sky,

A little nearer than I want it to be, but there it is,

With its half-mast current of stars.

Your new son is days from being born,

And the sun floats like a pastel lure beyond the offing,

71

And the Connecticut River is lovely again below us,
And the rains are suddenly breaking
Above Protestant Northampton,
And the Yiddish books
Crack open their borscht belt wisdom:

> *Always send a lazy man for the Angel of Death.*
> *A penny is a lot of money—if you haven't got a penny.*
> *Cancer, schmancer!—as long as you're healthy.*
> *Dear God: You do wonderful things for other people.*
>
> *Why not for me?*

In the next town over, Emily Dickinson is asleep for the season,
And Jonathan Edwards, too, is sound asleep as in death.
Your boy is sleeping inside the womb of his mother.
And my boy sleeps dreamily with his feet on the dashboard,
Sleeps dreamily with his bluesman's mop of hair
Soft as a nest, a little snoring, curled,
Waiting to be born into manhood and yon friendship.
Sleep, my son. Sleep. Sleep.

TO SNYDER FROM THE BLUE SCORCHER CAFÉ

—Astoria, Oregon

Dear Gary—

    Suddenly, in a town like this, you hear a man

At the next table say, he was "just thinking the other day

About Vishnu and Shiva," as he eats a bowl of lettuce.

I was just thinking the other day about Mount St. Helens

And your letter about how, thirty years on

After the volcano, the natural systems are teeming

Above sterile gravel and mudbanks.

                     "What's time to a pig?" you ask.

And Ursula talking about Artemis who is not exactly a virgin

But must go every year to a deep pool in the mountains

Where her virginity is magically renewed—

                     Artemis's, I mean.

So: Diversity equals stability and sustainability—

Like here where the gulls don't fade

But keep coming off the bridge,

Soundless at first, unceasing,

              as if transformed from the dead,

Then alighting over the waves.

Then: Diving into the waters

With the sunlight as fanfare in their wings,

And with the distance trailing in their flight

Back up to the bridge

             above the fast-moving bare-lipped

Mouth of the Columbia River

And the gummed-up fog

Until nothing is close to them but mute wonder.

    "Which is the trouble," the leathery fisherman

I dreamed about last night said in the dream.

I expect he's Finnish, too, because he also said,

"One should not go farther than the sea to fish."

                              Gary, I can't tell you

Whether he was a gill-netter or a cannery worker,

Bar pilot or deckhand, ship's cook or skipper.

But I can tell you that off these piers, in 1961, the cutter *Triumph*

Set out to rescue the *Mermaid* and hardly anyone survived.

There's a poem about it

Chiseled into a squall-gray maritime memorial:

> *The call of the* Mermaid *took them on out*
>
> *To the bleak afternoon of a January sea.*
>
> *We're taking on water, came the dim shout.*
>
> *And the spit called the peacock hard alee.*

Gary, I do not know if the fisherman in the dream

Was a longshoreman or drag fisherman,

A captain or a fisherman's son,

                              but now I do know the names

Of a handful of vessels sunk off this estuary:

The *Betty*, the *Silverside*,

The *Margaret*, the *Gypsy Lady*,

                              the *Princess*, the *Argo*,

And the *Garda Marie*, the *Daphne*, the *Maestro*,

The *Alma*, the *Viking Queen* —

Sunk in the graveyard waters

                    off Cape Disappointment

With its lighthouses winking at

Two-thousand-hours-a-year of fog.

And when I think of those names —

As if the names are hours in the wind and hours in the waters —

I think of lines from a Scottish ballad I have loved

And memorized more than once:

> *And mony was the feather bed*
>
> *That flatter'd on the faem;*
>
> *And mony was the gude lord's son*
>
> *That never mair cam hame.*

74

Gary, the Chinese say, "The best time to plant a tree
Was twenty years ago. The second best time is today."
I suppose that's why this is a town that doesn't sleep.
The river races along, and the bright grasses rise.
The fishmongers anchor at the espresso bars.
The *nouveau* have moved close to the iron works.
The one-car trolley brought over from Slovenia
Ding-dings along the new jogging path.
The mornings begin in fog and end in sun.
And the men live in burlap sacks.
And the women live with bread and creosote and rage.
It's a small dreary city — but you've heard that before.
Nobody takes a breather, and always the sky
Is collapsing into the hills
                    (mating, is what I want to say),
And is revealed in foamy lurches
The way shadows reveal the afterlife
Or mist becomes a lullaby —

> *So here's to our surf men, and brave airmen, too.*
> *Nor valor nor daring do they lack.*
> *Here's to the* Triumph *and her gallant crew.*
> *They went out, but they didn't come back.*

Last night, Gary, the tide rose so high
I thought the waves would splash through the doors,
And the Finnish adventurer came into my dreams
And corrected the way I said sauna —

                    it's *souw-na*

Like sow's ear, like sow's purse, like sow's ass.
Make no mistake, Gary, to a Finn the pronunciation matters!
So now I know that even though we can be knowledgeable
About the knowledge of other men,
We can't be wise with the wisdom of other men.
Therefore: I have learned to speak without whim,
But in doing so, I have unlearned watching things —

Sunlight in the trees, last leaves that quicken,
The quaint monotonous bark of gulls,
Brusque flowers on faded roadsides,
                        wounds of the half-sleep,
The swept half-wounds of the awakened.
I have unlearned all that,
                        as if every night
My mouth is a place where only darkness is spoken.
Trust me, so far as the volcano goes,
I won't breathe a word about the difference
Between a treated recovery and a wild process
So the loggers won't cut more trees than their share.
But I will say that in 1637, when Edward King
Dies in his passage from Chester on the Irish seas,
And John Milton writes —

> *Weep no more, woful Shepherds, weep no more,*
> *For Lycidas your sorrow is not dead,*
> *Sunk though he be beneath the watry floar,*
> *So sinks the day-star in the Ocean bed —*

All of English poetry changed.
So I want to believe the ocean has a language
As this river speaks in dreams.
And as I look over the sunset skies
With the cormorants and gulls like small guesses
Over the waves, and the Columbia River
                        deep and dirty with portent,
Undeified, and then recoiling
In a night of claws where the throats cry out,
I can only speak the lines I have myself not written —
As I write this letter to mark the hour:

> *O lang, lang may the ladies sit,*
> *Wi' their fans into their hand,*
> *Before they see Sir Patrick Spens*
> *Come sailing to the strand!*

76

And lang, lang may the maidens sit
Wi' their gowd kames in their hair,
A-waiting for their ain dear loves!
For them they'll see nae mair.
Half-owre, half-owre to Aberdour,
'Tis fifty fathoms deep;
And there lies gude Sir Patrick Spens
Wi' the Scots lords at his feet!

No one is home now, Gary.
Death takes the ones we do not want taken.
I will say that this day has four more hours of light
And then, two hours later, it's midnight.
The tankers strum back and forth to the quay.
Summer croons deeply, like fear and doubt.
And the bridge from this state to that one
Is so much like a prayer,
Like a hard shine we can't see
Flicking in and out with the wind,
A hard shine that disappears
Between thought and afterthought,
Between bridge and Paradise,
Aloft, ripening, greenest in the sun,
A long, trailing, magical spirit over the river
And the people who work it,
Veiling and unveiling the lives of the surfmen
Who go out and come back
As their women mythologize their wait on the shore
Along with the boats that carry them back and forth —
The *Blackthorn* and the *Savage Chief,*
The *Sunrise* and the *Johnny,* the *Seneca,* the *Bye Bye.*
And if the bridge could entangle the flesh,
                    it would entangle the flesh.
And if it could feel compassion, it would feel compassion.
And if it could dream all spirits into renewal —

Well, you've heard it before—hearts would dissolve
And be reborn, again and again, like the river.
Think about it, Gary, as Dick Hugo says. Be nice. Be well.

·

TO SYLVESTER FROM TERMINAL B

—George H. W. Bush Airport

—Houston, Texas

Dear Phil—

    I have always loved this terminal—

Even as a boy I roamed its lunar-lander halls,

And I never got over my happiness

With the crazy story of jet travel,

Never misunderstood how, from East Texas,

No one ever sees the ocean, nor honestly misses

Not seeing the ocean, what with the way our heat rises

In waves over the asphalt neighborhoods

                         and half-irrational trees,

What with the way our 254 counties

Seem always to have a whiff of uncertainty

Hanging above them, a sway

Of star-glitter that is part shine and part phewy,

And the way, too, I can't help but stroll

Inside these curvaceous hallways

Pleased as a poet among the daffodils!

And how every time I pass through this city,

I can't help but remember, too, that night

Outside Ruggles in Montrose—

One brother and I took to the parking lot after the beignets,

And he taught me "Leaving on a Jet Plane,"

                   two squeakers in the throes

Of a bad song that has a good heart.

                   You know,

I'm leaving on a jet plane. Don't know

When I'll be back again. Oh, babe, I hate to go.

What was my brother saying to me back then,

                   when neither of us had grown

Into manhood, when in that moment we could almost believe
Something was waiting for us in the future
Beyond the boom-chica-chica melodies of our Tex-Mex city
Where only in the burrito sheds could you find someone
To speak of war who might know that there is little difference
Between dying for your country and killing for your country?
Phil, any age is just so new.

                                   I'll tell you this:
What's new in Terminal B is the 8-foot-tall bronze sculpture
Of the 41st President of the United States
Who adopted oily Midland and did OK, sure,
And whose second son you already know, your roommate
During the dire year you went to Phillips Academy—
The future governor of Florida, your homey!
Like everyone else in Terminal B,
The 41st President of the United States is in an 8-foot-tall hurry.
He's windswept with the winds of change,
His tie blowing heroically over the left shoulder,
His jacket held vibrantly over the other shoulder,
A hustling bronze man
Hustling into a lone wind, some book in hand, too,
And his face taut with an unscoured vision—

                              an 8-foot-tall bronze saint
Is what you're supposed to feel when you stare up at his great
Great greatness! Something in the mind
Splits in half in moments like that,
As if one part of the brain cannot find the other part,
And Part A does not miss Part B,
And the contexts of humanity are lost
And what are to be found in the details are details,
And what are to be made from the details are also details.
Phil, I wish that statue had been dedicated to the Almighty
As a kind of slithery baptism wrestled out of a wildcatter.
Or, say, the 8-foot-tall bronze president is headed to the Bacchanalia!

With dancing maidens and cafés opened until eternity!
And the cathedrals straight as swords!
And every murmur comprehended by every stone!
And yet, when you look around Terminal B,
You see, for all the world, that everyone must come home to die.
I wonder: Is it the cloud-thick sky they need?
The white air that tightens over the decaying bodies?
Here's what my Houstonians need to know
About the man inside the statue:
On the evening of his great loss in 1992,
Somewhere past midnight, he wrote in his diary
That defeat "hurt, hurt, hurt...." Then—

> *Comfort the ones I've hurt and let down.*
> *Finish with a smile and some gusto.*

—Phil, not long after that night of singing,
My brother and I tried to plant a garden
In the fenced-in backyard on Loch Lomond Drive
About thirty miles from here,
And very little grew for a couple of Yiddish farmers

aged four and nine.

It was as if we were trying to plant our own names
Into the Texas earth
With the months humid
Even inside the tines of the rakes.
I guess we wanted to grow something

so as to carry our work

Into whatever travels lay ahead, whatever worries
Were to come along, come and go.
We furrowed, we dug, we seeded, we waited,

and sometimes watered—

Spinach bolted. Tomatoes cracked. And the cucumbers.
And the days went by with a wind we should have called *forbid,*
And the years went by with a wind we didn't call anything.
What can I say? What can I say?

We were nameless boys

Flowing straight up for years and then straight down —

And, in one city after another,

In phases of wandering into and out of lives,

We went in search of other brothers,

And we found them, too, from time to time,

And we added their singing to ours.

Sometimes, Phil, when the sun dims,

Taking nothing and giving nothing,

When the sun dims in a southwestern sky

Like this one, in August, in the unremodeled airport

                     with its Moon Shot décor,

The sterile blossoms of a brotherly garden

Unfold in portraits of passing faces,

Men and women of every consequence,

As if they are chalked and erased with charcoal —

And they unfold inside distant brothers, too,

And in parents, and then parents that die.

Even when we expect death to come,

We are not ready when it does —

No, we are not ready, as we are seldom ready

When the sun etches out of the sky,

And the weeds we have not picked purr higher.

And the ocean two-thousand-five-hundred miles from here

Survives in its embers,

The ocean calling in the believers

With their fists thrust at the stars,

Their knuckles like honeycombs,

The believers straggling into the low waves,

And the sun-stunned winds blowing every which way.

      Phil, the Romans say, in wine there is truth.

OK then, I'm for wine!

           Especially here

In Bubba's Bar and Grill inside Terminal B!

Here, the podunks and bumbershoots,
The abdicators and the yiddle men
All get to have their say.
What I hear now is a lady with a two-step drawl
Calling my flight!
Look, I'll be leaving soon.
Even with all the brothers I've added,
I'm still missing one — gone out to find the wind
And we don't know when he's coming back.
That's not fate, that's the Book of Life's child

      singing in silence.
I write to hear, you draw to hear, a brother prays to hear.
But once — I almost heard that other brother!
And then I almost understood
How chance bleeds into the earth.
There's more to say, Phil, but the lady is calling my flight.
Sometimes it just feels bitter saying goodbye so often.
A few army recruits are loitering in the bookstalls.
Brothers of somebody.

    We cannot save them, Phil,
Not with poetry, not with art,

   nor with the songs of boys

   nor the prayers of men.
One dies, another is born,
And the wreck of the heart unwrongs those we love.
We live in a world of matter and creatures

    and unmemorized power.
Just boys, Phil.
Sometimes with the wind at their backs,
Other times a wind in their faces.
Just boys, passing through home.

TO GIFFORD FROM UNITED FLIGHT 308

— Portland to Greensboro

Dear Giff—

    Dawn-dark, then lift-off, and suddenly

The plane nosing above the pioneer clouds,

And now I have to remember that down there

                           is not my land.

Even if I shut my eyes, nothing appears or disappears.

Shut my eyes, and nothing can stop the baby in the row one over

From gurgling—as nothing can better conjure the dusty meaning

Of cattlemen, logging towns, and wagon roads—

As nothing can puncture the ends of those rivers

That slant and scramble out of the old forests.

And: While I believe we are all Texans now,

Oregon, says Wendy, is disputed territory—

I must see later today how the Kashmiri are getting on!

What else to do but look through this capsule of a window

At the high desert and then, as if at once, Idaho, Wyoming,

The hours like seconds—

               then the Rockies, purified and ajar

And darkening into the brown haze of the valleys.

Now bits of pleasant snow in the higher passes,

              bits of wind

Cutting up two lone, spare clouds,

              a wisp and a whiling away,

The sun already afloat where I'm headed.

Same goes for life in general, yes, Giff?

              Afloat, I mean.

Where ideas and musings ridge upward into our sights

And make sense even as they change over history and time?

And, on the other hand, over all that time,

The landscape of the inner life remains constant.

Right?

And, if the inner life is constant, our affliction
Must be most with the ways we humans kill —
I mean, we are eclipsed with killing ourselves,
Murmur and murmur of killing, and forgotten killing,
Our murderous sanctuaries we glorify and forbear.
And what might that mean to the newlyweds across the aisle,
She with her page-boy hair,
He with his shaved head on her shoulder,
She dozing restlessly, and now she's stirring.
What valley in the psyche must they reconcile?
It's unlikely that tonight they will sleep
Under the skins of the buffalo.
And so — this is how I while away the time up here! —
I say they will not sleep with death.
But they must live with death as we all must.
Believe me, I understand their struggle
Up here in seat 32C because, with the air flatly eminent,
It's getting harder to stay in accord with nature!
                         This is a bumpy cabin, Giff —
A bit of ginger ale now — *thank you, my dear* — for the queasiness.
And if the pilot doesn't find a smoother ride soon,
I may have to quit this bleached-out letter.
And yet, let me at least share this:
Kitty-corner from me there's an auntie with a perm.
She's sleeping with the Good Book open on her lap.
And while she may be snoring through Solomon 2:11,
Those newlyweds would be wise to have a look:

> *For lo, the winter is past, the rain is over and gone;*
> *The flowers appear on the earth;*
> *The time of the singing of birds is come,*
> *And the voice of the turtle is heard in our land;*
> *The fig tree putteth forth her green figs,*
> *And the vines with the tender grape give a good smell.*

85

Giff, up here, a new era of unreality is only beginning.

But, below,

I can see America is all bedrooms and barrooms,

Shacks and stripped trees and hand-me-down desires,

Crazy little backyard pools and man-made malls,

Crowds and crowds of workmen, and what I can only imagine

To be a sunburnt prairie boy north of Galveston

Somewhere (maybe right below!) who, not so taciturn,

Gives his whole heart to anyone who will take him.

He's filled with gifts of praise and waiting for his school bus,

And now I imagine he stomps the katydids.

How I want him to see the years to come

As a dwelling place in time,

As if dwelling inside the self,

Inseparable as sun from moon,

As window from the eyes.

And yet it must be the stormy weather

that's spurred us

Suddenly over the Gulf of Mexico —

where, down on NASA Road 1,

There exist the good shrimp huts and crawfish rooms of my childhood.

Heavens, I say, the land is the land and we work it hard.

Meanwhile, we have arrived over Texas in the year of our year

And what we have to say to each other, Giff, is *one* this,

And *zero* that, as if *one* and *zero* are the finer codes

for understanding existence,

As if *one* and *zero* reveal pity and love,

An idiosyncratic God, a self-improved God.

But, Giff, those old hangouts of mine on NASA Road 1,

I miss them.

And now, just like that, with a double-bump and a skid,

We're on the ground in a Harris County rain.

— So let me pause, again,

To thank the God of my choice for Terminal B!

86

And for landing safely in my own land!
                              The glorious space age hallways,
A hot bowl of chili at Bubba's,
Strolling over to Gate 27,
                              and just like that,
We're back in the sky above the parishes of Louisiana.
                              But, look!
Little auntie is here! She's awake!
And, her hair is holding up!
And, lo, she is flipping through the pages of the Good Book—
Tell us, auntie, please, what is it Jesus says
About the Kingdom to come and how the world will end?
Auntie, does Jesus say it will come by expectation?
God, I hope not.
35,000 feet above the yawp-yawp
                              Confederate ditches,
I want to know that He says that the Kingdom of God
Is already spread upon the Earth,
And the men and women and children just do not see it.
Perhaps a little poem, a painting, a beautiful lesson
In a schoolroom, a splendid fiddle-riff
So surprising even the violinist has tears coming on,
                              or even a letter like this one—
All of it meant to make the inner and outer existences visible.
Such is the manner—I'm guessing here!—
That consciousness informs itself.
                              Or, I don't know.
Whatever. What I know is, outside the airplane's window
It's dappled clouds. What the painterly touches mean
I have no idea or, if I did, I will soon forget.
In every direction clouds are gathering,
Staining the upper air above the Southern borders.
Let's call *that* transcendence
                    for your old friend now in seat 7A.

87

But, what's beyond that, Giff?

And, as I look deeply out the window

At the wing and distant clouds,

                    what is beyond the beyond?

Let me guess: There's no name for it.

Because there's no name for knowledge

That the tongue has not tasted.

I hear you wanting to say:

                    That's the mystical, man.

Then say it.

Say the eternal is within.

Say time is the devil.

Say it, and then what?

And does saying it turn these dappled clouds into a white shrine?

And what must be said of the country down there?

America, can you give us what we need?

America, is there a long straw?

America, why has your shadowy nightmare

Given us villagers with torches

Who march in a hundred rows?

All morning, I've looked for a clear sign through windows

That do not reveal the self and do not reveal the other.

I sit where I sit. Meantime, across the aisle,

                    Jesus is in the lap of the auntie.

There's sky-light above me and sky-light below

Like the form and structure of living and being alive.

Today, at least, I'm good

With the God of Arrivals and the God of Departures.

Yea! That He comes and goes on time!

And for all the bruised and strung-out clouds,

For all the picked-clean air

And the last nuggets of ice on the tongue,

I seal this for you in my blue knapsack under the seat in front of me,

Seal it as we descend, seal it as the sky licks its shadows.

Later tonight, this jet will have landed, taken off,

and landed again,

Back and forth, like a craze, across the nation,

And the wheels will have rolled to a stop

and gone hush,

And, in the small city among the slow living

Where I will set my bags down for a few nights,

The stars, as they do, will coldly slide out,

And I will stand barefoot in the dewy grass

And, like a boy in search of other places,

Listen for a single cricket in the dark.

TO C. D. FROM D.C.

— Washington, D.C.

Dear Carolyn—

      All week we have walked in front of the Old
Executive Office building on Pennsylvania Avenue
And across the asphalt White House plaza,
And we have waved to the half-starved protester
In Lafayette Park as he stood ten steps
From where Walt Whitman used to stand,
Not in such great shape himself, the old coot,
When he would wave to Abe Lincoln
As he rode out alone on horseback
On summer evenings in 1863,
Trotting his tallest horse to the Soldier's Home
Above the Rock Creek, to sleep on the land
Where the first Civil War cemetery was put.
Can you imagine the Great Emancipator
Standing on his back porch among the dead
As he listened to the diggers graveling the graves,
Chipping the soil, lifting in the bodies,
From Rochester and Groton and Poolesville
And King of Prussia, lifting in the bodies
With the steam rising from their skins
Into the insect-mating womb of the light
Around the city, the utterly still bodies
                        unquivering?
You had asked what was it like to live here
Twenty-five years ago—Carolyn,
Truth be told, I was drunk
So much of the time I cannot say.
I can say it was a city of saviors,
That's for sure, powder-cheeked and God awful,

The street corners like hospital sheets,
The 15th Street pimps chatting

              with the newsmen from the *Post*,
The dreadlocked couriers quick and mingling
With the FCC guys, the diplomats
Slumping *cum laude* without their blue blazers
Across Foggy Bottom, the portable flags
Dropping their stars underneath the partisan air,
And the New England legislators — in their socks
After hours at the Irish pubs near Union Station —
Like dome-shadowed columns
Of dreamers with the eyes of animals
And a meeting in an hour on Embassy Row,
And the ex-officio in Dupont Circle
With one eye on his German beer
And another on the crowds — "See her,
That's the wife of the Belgian
Ambassador's chief of staff" — and the poets
Sneaking into matinees of *Lawrence of Arabia*
At the Uptown, then wandering through Rock Creek Park
Listening for linnets, speaking of a thousand things,
As John Keats says one must, and so the talk
Would broach nightingales and sensations,
Genera and species of fancy,
The loose quadrants between will and volition,
Metaphysics and consciousness, monsters,
Mermaids, good morning, and good night —
And all that time we could not see the airy
Path of Abraham Lincoln

                   who rode his tallest horse
Into those very woods — he must have enjoyed
Dipping swiftly into the bliss and dizzy
Hungers of the night — so much to love
In this city, so much to hold up to the world,

The 19th century streets, even now, rumbling
Behind the crabapple trees, every brick house
Stacked with its hatreds and adorations,
And the parkway shimmering

              back into the lettered avenues —
And, yes, I still love the bridges, Carolyn,
That cross into Arlington in Northern Virginia
Onto Robert E. Lee's sloping lawn
With its milky headstones,
And, better, a mile or so further on,
The red neon "EAT" sign that hung
Above Whitey's for fifty years
And now is gone, a juke joint that popped
With broasted chicken and unconnoisseur
Beers and *diddly-diddly* players —
With a deer's head nailed to the wall
Next to a photograph of a goose-eyed TR,
A place where I once bumped into a general
At eight o'clock and a senator at midnight.
What I was drinking those days remains
A mystery, those years a long body
Of rain poured into a short glass, gentle rain
Like the odor of earth plowed in and upturned,
Rain like the willowy church bells on Sunday,
Rain like the faces in apartment windows,
Rain like the bodies tipped into the ground,
Rain like a wife and home that would last
And, then, in the end, not last —
A bad-mannered, good-natured honky-tonk,
Whitey's was a hole,
A pickup hall, a chuck wagon, a giddy-up,
Where a man pissed in the Gent's Room
And threw darts in the Lincoln Room,
So inspirational in the lore of those times

A local personal read:
"Intense, creative professional,
36, 6 ft. 3 in. tall,
220 lbs on a large frame,
Seeks a confident, yet compliant, buxom
S/D/WF, 25–40, who can handle herself
At Embassy receptions as well as at Whitey's."
Living here was like that, all squint and chortle.
And the blind justice downriver
Carefully fingered like a four-cornered fold.
And the no-fault talk of the town folk
Confided on napkins at the Tabard Inn.
And the accidental grace that the tourists bring
As they come in buses from across
The plinky shared heart of America
And step onto Constitution Avenue,
And breathe hard, and dream of freedom.
All of it mixed with the frumpy Armanis
And *mmm-mmm* ladies that work the shifts.
Walking these boulevards with you, Carolyn,
The last few days — the two of us Southerners
With sympathies, you a hill country
                     daughter of Arkansas
Me an immigrant's lost son who grew up
In the the shaded lawns of Harris County, Texas,
Chatting about the textbooks we handled
                in public school,
Called *The Lost Cause and the Republic*,
Called *Abraham Lincoln and His War*,
Called *Still Fighting*, and you wondering
If you'll ever get back to Baxter County
Now that your parents have died
And there's not a good cup of coffee
To be had there, and if one more body says,

"Bless you, Carolyn," you'll slit your white throat—
Walking these boulevards, what can I say, I feel joy!
Even now, I want to loaf in Lafayette Park
And sleep in the recesses of the Rock Creek
And watch the stars sequester in the shuttered sky.
I want to search for a grainy Walt Whitman
Among the lunch counters and mope with him
Over the beautiful eyes of Abraham Lincoln—
So this morning, at dawn, in a staggered light,
Among the sharp Marine Corps joggers
And administrative assistants in skirts,
I wandered out and stood near
The fisted hand of the 16th president
As he sat in marble along the Potomac River,
And I read his great American poems,
And, what can I say, I felt at home.
Though I know some anger is called for.
Across the land, I know, there are poisonous
Billboards and simplified infantries,
Half a million children gently swallow
Their antipsychotic pills, the slathery
Bicycle chains of Southeast Portland
And the six-geared lawn mowers of Dallas
Do not abide, nor the sad Dairy Queens
Of Detroit or the dog-eared menus
At the Peking Noodle Parlor in Butte.
The Society of Clowns will not dance
With the basement full of Marxists
At their back-to-back early morning meetings
In the Mission Splendor of Christ Church in San Jose.
None of it abides. Or this: In Warsaw,
Ohio, on most Saturday nights,
The God-fearing sweet parishioners
From the New Beginnings Ministry

Gather in front of the Fox Hole strip club
And photograph the dancers as they come
To work, and they put the girls' faces
On posters in the town green. But then,
Come Sunday mornings, the strippers don't despair.
They congregate outside New Beginnings
In their bikinis!
              And, with squirt guns,
They souse their bodies with glee and sing hymns
And dance and come holy and praise the Lord.
                      Sure, I've prayed for exile, too —
Though now, Carolyn, as I think of us
                    crossing the plaza
In front of the White House from east to west,
As if from Maine to California,
You are talking about your father
Dying so soon after your mother,
And your son fighting and loving into life,
And the torrents of art and the thunder
And the creepy beautiful deep,
And you have the look of a woman
Whose heart has gone out to the end of a rope
And your eyes shimmer with metalwork faith
And blindness, and you believe the nation
Is being murdered, that even the horses
Of Virginia are turning Republican.
So what is there to say about those years?
Once, in the groaning hour before dawn,
Bob Farnsworth and I climbed a cherry tree
Behind the brick horseshoe apartments
Of the Freud Hilton some two miles
From the President's bed, and for an hour
Or so — I cannot tell a lie
When it comes to cherries, who can! — we stole

A dozen butter-tubs full of the cherries
From the topmost branches of another man's tree.
We'd shimmied up without ladders
                              in the late spring air,
And the heart-shaped cherries wept into our hands.
I remember it now, if memory
Has anything to do with it: We'd come
Stumbling good as God out of Whitey's
After defending the pool table for rounds
And drinking as many in whiskey,
And what I remember is, each cherry
Seemed like an eye unstaring at the ground,
The darkling ground, the easeful ground,
Twenty feet below where the sidewalks slanted
Toward the elegant Duke Ellington Bridge,
And I began to understand that life
In this district is all or nothing.
I wanted to say this to you earlier,
Carolyn, as we were lazily walking
Into the National Gallery,
But I could see that the black-and-white snapshots
By the Paterson, New Jersey, poet
                              of the law firm
Of Ginsberg, Kerouac, Burroughs, Cassidy, and Corso
Could not change a thing if I did.
You stood in the gallery with your pocketbook
Over your shoulder, and looked into the eyes
Of the poets and saw the poets of your own life
Stare back — they'd jumped or hung or drowned,
All heroic and pink and ravishing
With scribble and splatter and airy
Instinct and ecstasy. But they could not
Change a thing. The poets die, and they die.
A mother dies, and then a father,

And all the worrying about boys
Who take to the streets with wildness and sinew.
And all the while I can only speak
Of the cherries from 1989,
And it changes nothing.

                              Yet, suddenly,
In the very moment of changelessness,
Bob, waddling a few branches below me
(I had clambered to the higher limbs
As if straddling the sky), begins to whistle
"You Run Deep in Me," then sings it:

> Oh, I may wander, but when I do
> I will never be far from you.
> You're in my blood and I know you'll always be,
> Arkansas, you run deep in me.

What a Mainiac like him was doing singing
The state song of Arkansas, I'll never know!
"I like the state songs," he said when I asked him.
"All of them?"
"That one."
"I can't stand 'Texas, Our Texas,'" I said.
I said, "I like 'The Eyes of Texas Are Upon You.'"
"Not a state song," he said.
Then belted out Maine's into the sky of the capital city,

> Oh, Pine Tree State
> Your woods, fields and hills
> Your lakes, streams and rockbound coast
> Will ever fill our hearts with thrills
> And tho' we seek far and wide
> Our search will be in vain
> To find a fairer spot on earth
> Than Maine! Maine! Maine!

Carolyn, I will come to the point:
We went on picking cherries like that,

Bob moving from border to border,
From "Home on the Range" to "Sewanee River,"
From "On the Banks of the Wabash"
To "Georgia on My Mind," from "Yankee Doodle"
To "I Love New York," from "Oklahoma"
To "Carry Me Back to Old Virginia."
He sang, I hummed, and the cherries came
Softly into our hands. But we did not meet
Abe Lincoln that night in the seamy
Alleys north of the Potomac River.
And we did not dine with Walt Whitman.
And we did not turn back in time at Gettysburg,
And we did not find Oswald soon enough.
And we did not think how inappropriate
Or otherwise appropriate for America
The name Whitey's was for a dive in old Virginia.
And fiery Allen Ginsberg of New Jersey
Who took photographs of his best friends
Did not weep with us as he does
In the self-portrait from the hotel bathroom
With its wall-to-wall mirrors,
In which his naked body rumples
Over and over toward the last century,
And you said, "He's really quite tender,
Allen is, in that one."
                    So I will speak of that —
Of the galloping rain in the heart,
Of scaling the familial wilds,
Of the limestone statues with their pulp
And proclamations, of the roughs at Whitey's
And listening to the blur of the dead,
Of the poets in the libatious, grainy,
Lunatic land, of the swirls and sifting
And springtime on the tongue.

                                      And of you
In windy Rhode Island now, far from home.
— We scabbered up the cherry tree
And stole the cherries, and we took them
To our women and, one by one, we pried
The cherries open and lifted each heart
Into our mouths, and we dipped the liquor
Of the nation into our mouths, and we
Proclaimed ourselves satisfied, and we rejoiced.

TO UNRAU FROM UNION

—West Virginia

Dear Don—

      Since you are in Hanoi for the city's
1,000th anniversary, taking portraits
Of cockfights and leftover bomb casings,
Men in barbershops and daughters
In rice fields and schoolyards,
And late night drinking
Before the monsoons come,
                    I will write to you
To say that in West Virginia—where we
White folk arrived in 1671—
Over 40 percent of the adults
Are missing one or more of their teeth ("No!"
Says Wendy from the other room, "It's 6
Or more!") Also, 75 percent
Of the young people who leave the state
Never come back. And yet, here we are,
With the skewed light of autumn
Cutting into the slow mountains.
          And, glory to us, too, Don,
It's election season!
This morning in the front lot of the I.G.A.,
We met Clyde Gum, Jr., who is running
For Monroe County Commissioner.
He looks like a second-string outside linebacker,
Shakes my hand more fey than I expect,
With a sweet grin, and his ball cap pulled low,
Two days unshaven, and he thanks us for shopping—
So I promise to vote for him, and I would
If I lived in Monroe County, West Virginia!

I mean, I love Clyde now! And cheer for days
When I see his candy-apple-red signs straddling
The creek sides and fence posts.
I hope he can do something about the teeth, Don.

                       I mean, at the I.G.A.
We bought two Roma tomatoes,
A bag of green grapes, and one cucumber,
Each shrink-wrapped in plastic.
Some fried chicken made behind the case,
Jerky, licorice—and that's about all
The fresh food there was.
The wispy lady behind us with three boys
Under seven underfoot had a cart
Filled with two dozen cans of pop,
Little Debbie Donuts, frozen Eggos,
Thirteen cans of Chef Boyardee,
Five cans of Chicken of the Sea,

                     and so many
Swanson's dinners I can't count without her
Noticing—and right now I'm trying not to stare.
Wendy looks like she's about to cry—
So there's this: Back in the parking lot
You could see that everyone has avoided
Grieving and gawking at the meek—
And there's little interest in foreign hand cream

                     or handmade jewelry
Or debutantes or lanky brats
Who understand the schisms of Christ.
And yet, still, the paperweights on aisle nine
Glisten in the artificial light,
And some thunder growls back of the hills,
And the gentle believers have not given up
On loneliness. And the money, someone says
To Clyde, will soon be cut loose.

And the afternoon flickers its light
Like bare twigs snapping into evening.
That was Union, Don. I hope Clyde Gum, Jr.,
Knows already that anyone who is
Popular is bound to be disliked.
Meantime, we've come to watch the year fade
And to consider love and solitude —
For instance, there is this painting
Of a two-storey red house with a creek
And a waterwheel, white and black ducks
Wading into the shallows,
Four cows dipping into the water,
                    cooling their hooves,
An abandoned skiff, slow easy pools,
Brown leaves in the air,
Bare-but-painterly branches,
And on the decrepit footbridge,
A young boy leaning close to a fine girl
With a bonnet. With so much bucolic joy,
One might forget about the coalfields!
                  — Wendy says
Coal was first discovered here
300 years ago in 1742 in Boone County.
She says more than half
Of the nation's electricity runs on coal.
She says that slurry in the water
And dust in the air are killing West Virginians
So slowly people are able not to notice.
She says for every 1,400 pounds of coal
Produced in a county, hospitalizations
In that county increase by 1 percent.
Boone County produces 6.6 million pounds a year.
— Don, I must tell you
This is not the poetical part of the poem.

This is the statistical part.—
I was about to tell you
About the painting on the wall
Where the boy is regaling his girl
                              with stories
About the ghost of the bewildered crying infant
And the ghost of the lost wife,
About the lover's ghost
Locked in the O'Dell house in Greenville,
And the headless horseman of Powers Hollow
That told folks in dreams of burying
A pot of money during the Civil War,
And when they'd try digging it up,
They'd come upon the pot,
Come upon it in the ground,
But as soon as they reached for it,
The pot would sink deeper into the earth.
Now the ghost rider on Highway 33.
Now the phantom wagon.
Now the woman in white.
Now the errant husband.
And, finally, the peddler's ghost
Near the Kanawha River—
                    where, in the McLung house,
A peddler was killed one winter night
                              and the bloodstains
Could still be seen behind the doors for years
And years and nothing could remove them,
And even when new owners removed the boards
And replaced them, the bloodstains returned.
And then one night there were sounds from the house
And people came to hear it, and one man called,
"Come out and show yourself!"
And then, just then, footsteps.

And a rattle at the doorknob.

But they saw nothing. No one.

But I do not want to tell you about that one, Don.

You know about ghosts, don't you?

Surely, you think, "Yes, Dave,

                  I know about ghosts.

They can be found

On the Giai Phong Road to Hanoi" —

Spare, unredeemed, untranslatable,

Like a stomach wound from 1969.

Like misunderstanding love.

Like shoving memory and quarrels

Into pockets so deep your hands ache.

Don, I hope Clyde can pull it out!

Election Day is a week and a half off.

What will he do without even one lump

Of coal to be dug up in Monroe County?

                  These are muddling days, Don,

Days to putter through the dim luck,

Or the cold, or the rain,

Where the odor of woodburn

Is as good to me as a quest for cosmic dust.

Who is not ready to die for the forgotten, Don?

Who is not ready? Moon-eyed and carrying our flag?

TO LENNEY FROM THE GREENBRIER HOTEL

—White Sulphur Springs, West Virginia

Dear Dinah—

There are days like this one, with the wind stripping the barks of trees
And the old light crinkling into a cool regiment of the afternoon,
When it's easy to forget where the wounds of the South have come from.
There are days like this one
When I'm staggering into the afternoon chill,

egged on with the last gist of the gin.

Days like this one that I've almost put a hand to those wounds
As one puts a hand across a lesion to stop the blood.
But then, nothing.
They are, after all, just wounds.
Bark to a tree. Smoke to a fire.

—In 1868, Robert E. Lee

Signed the White Sulphur Manifesto at this hotel.
Not as famous as the Gettysburg Address, it proclaimed:

The idea that the Southern people are hostile to the negroes,
And would oppress them
If it were in their power to do so, is entirely unfounded.

As if history is not a scythe cutting down the weeds.
I mean, on the quick road here there's a farmhouse with an American flag
Raised next to a Confederate stars and bars—
Did our man not know West Virginia seceded

during the war to rejoin the Union?

Did you know that when Lee surrendered to Grant
He wore a snowy-gray tunic buttoned to the neck,

a red silk sash,

His sword buckled with an ornate hilt and scabbard?
He'd trimmed his gray beard and put on new spurs.
"I expect," Lee told aides,

"I shall be General Grant's prisoner in the morning."

All this happened about a hundred miles from here.
Lee arrived at one in the afternoon.

> Grant, at one-thirty,

Having come straight from the field,
Had borrowed a coat from a private.

> It was too small and fit tight.

His pants were mud-splattered,
Stuffed into mud-splattered boots.

> Without insignia or sword.

He looked like a fly, one observer said,

> on a shoulder of beef.

"I met you once before, sir," Grant began,
"While we were serving in Mexico.
I always remembered your appearance,
And I think I should have recognized you anywhere."

> "I have often thought of it," Lee answered,

"And tried to recollect how you looked,
But I have never been able to recall a single feature."

> —When it was done

And he had given in, Lee left first, stood,
A little dazed, on the stoop—
Union officers, waiting for the surrender,

> came to and saluted—

Lee donned his hat and returned the salute,
Raised his arm slowly to his forehead
As if pulling his hand up

> through air thick as honey,

Then snapped it downward

> as if to shake off water.

Grant ordered his men to mount Traveler,
And as the orderly brought the tall horse near,
The Virginian lifted the horse's forelock

> out from under the brow

And lightly patted the forehead in the manner,

it was said,

As one who loved horses but whose thoughts are far away.

Grant raised his hat to Lee — Lee raised his hat to Grant.

And then Robert E. Lee rode his white horse alone back to the men

He'd surrendered as prisoners to the Grand Army of the Republic.

That's how quietly the business ended, with hats

and hands

And the soft ears of a horse.

Dinah, once, in a hard Tennessee light,

A hundred and twenty years later,

I sought out the wounds I called REMEMBER.

I was standing along the Cumberland River

watching the moon's broken O

Rise above the water and the Fourth of July revelers,

And I was waiting for all the peacockery to start.

I was hardly alone but, still, I felt a quiet

surround me,

And something vague came over me

About the origins of cities

With their temples and marketplaces and commercial towers

And — hardened in between — the limestone

Government offices that are no longer

the center of American beauty

Or even craftsmanship, though mistresses

Still wait for their men at the top of the thick steps

In order to slip off and marry words to each other

About the lust and exhaustion and frailty in their bones.

But though I was among so many of my countrymen,

Just then I sought out the wounds

I called REMEMBER

And tried to tell myself again

The story of Lee surrendering to Grant

as I have told it to you.

But a churchy whistle sniggered back —

it began in the glottal hills of the throat

And ended with a hard blast through the mouth.

In the White Sulphur Manifesto, the Southerners write —

>   *Whatever opinions may have prevailed in the past*
>   *In regard to African slavery, or the right of a State*
>   *To secede from the Union, we believe we express*
>   *The almost unanimous judgment of the Southern people*
>
>   *when we declare*
>
>   *That they consider that those questions were decided by the war.*

Dinah, here, winter is coming on,

And with it sheets of gray clouds

Framing the branches with scraps of white.

                                I think of you in Los Angeles —

Where the century has turned autumn into a hazy rasp

And the Age of Reason remains in full bloom,

And the strobes and straggly halos of the red-lighted freeways

Do not prevent anyone from carrying in the milk,

Unwrapping the news or sleeping until noon.

              I mean: No matter the color, a dog is a dog.

— But, now, somewhere in the distances of West Virginia

I hear not bells but *Hallelujah! Hallelujah!*

And the rooftops seem to lift off,

                            and the black birds suddenly

Ascend under the sky. And the gentle *Hallelujahs*

Are wild and unsuspecting.

Who can understand the wounds that blur with joy?

And the wounds you've held? Or I have?

Those wounds are just mud now,

Part payday, part gaudy hotel.

Because even if a man could disown memory,

The wound would swell.

TO BIESPIEL FROM UNITED FLIGHT 1037

—Greensboro to Atlanta

Dear brother—

      I used to think of death all the time,
And then for a time I didn't, or didn't try to,
And now I do not expect to die on this flight
Above the skies from the Carolinas to Georgia,
Where, if I were to die, I would not have chosen Atlanta
What with its bad moods and old alchemies.
Therefore: No one will say your brother has died today.
He will not be clubbed in the aisle.
He will not fall out of the Trust-in-God skies

                      above the Tennessee valley.
Outside this airplane, it is Friday. It is dusk.
I imagine you bringing your son and daughter
Out of the failing light of Chicago
To praise bread and wine
And cover their small heads
So that they will not be abandoned.
Though I would suggest—up here where the air is a threat
And, at times, unkind to hard thought—
That a prayer for solitude and crooked rivers
Would do as well.

            But I am not that brother.
Nor am I the brother that has disremembered himself
The way the thousands of dead patches of farms
Rendered below across the slop of land
Have disremembered themselves—

                so many farms
Unwombed from the pace of the nation.
Even from here, you can see that their days
Go so slowly, too slowly,

Beneath the well-oiled tines of the tractor,
                    puckering and chuffing,
As they scratch at the Pentecostal stubble.
That brother fled into shreds of light.
He clutched no one's hand.
He dissolved as the sky dissolves.
Him like a dreadful night himself,
Jeering with a bulging howl.
And yet, how primal, that brother,
A prodigal swallow that comes back,
Convinced in the music to come
Under the garment-blue sky.
And now, as I look out the window
                    above Georgia
At the horizon's edge, a long flat red
Collapses, then bruises into a peachy white,
Then layers and layers swaying
                    into a sudden lace of white.
And, then, one stray star above Atlanta.
And now sharpening like a pressing gratitude.
And now the land a spongy dark, a plowed hush,
As if what's at the end of time is not regret and fury
But satisfaction and sweetness and stitched stars.

TO LUKE FROM UNITED FLIGHT 251

—Chicago to Portland

Sweetheart—

       Just now the moon unhid itself,
And the hours splayed
In every direction across the knuckled lands.
Those are mostly unused hours
Like unused chances, and they flood the future.
Up here, I acknowledge my status

                        as a distraught father.
Had I been able to grant you one thing for your life
It would not be beauty but friendship—
I mean, a natural friend who rises from stranger to intimate,
A kindhearted friend with a mind lit by ice and stars
Who brings to you just the right amount of trouble
To make the days bandy with plenty.
A grand friend for whom courtesy comes easy
Like rose and thistle, bedazzled and brute.
Let me give you that as a pedigree for your 18th year
With your face bearding into a fine splurge
And your Blind Willie voice calming the hearts
When you tilt back on the stages of dark cities
And bring the rising sun suffering out of your body:

       When the train left the station
       With the two lights on behind,
       The blue light was my blues,
       The red light was my mind.

I've been dozing on and off on this flight for an hour.
I can't say why but I've been thinking about sundials,
How they freeze after so much ticking,

                   and melt and vanish,
Every second dilating into long years

That suddenly get relinquished as a pensive dream
Where we are surprised to see a few dead men
From the sepia photographs of brother and uncles —
                              first from the dismantled
World of Europe that now looks like a forgery.
Later Harris County. Later the N Judah
                              delivering us
Not from evil but unto the foggy Ocean Beach.
And now a city rising in a rain of foliage.
I've been summoning all of that
                    like a flutter of mirrors.
That's one kind of compartment in my mind.
Another is filling up with a flurry of blackbirds.
They are, in this moment, in my mind, utter matter —
Submerging in shadows, shadowless themselves,
As if they represent everything I might have wished for
That has become unattainable,
The way desire is more strange without an object of desire.
                         You can try out scheming,
Luke, the artful will.
The projected coercion of craving for the vast.
You can try that. See how it goes.
You could root in that.
                    Then shred to pieces
And feel cruel, stained, ruined, and unknown.
Unknowable. The evidence come clean finally
In a fresh pandemonium of gratitude —
And there'll be nothing I could have done.
To fear change, Luke, is to fear the history and science
Of feeling (that's Wordsworth, read him).
But now as the lights of the airstrip crop up,
The uncounted, unaccountable blackbirds
                              assemble and fidget
And scatter and take off in tar-whipped squadrons,

Sharpen and circle and veer and steadily
Bawl and cry upward to liquefy as the wild.
And the streets are left finite in their sooty dark,
Left sodden in the electrified miles.

TO WENDY FROM THE CROW'S NEST

— Portland

My dear—
        If not from dream, before dawn,
When the rain has not perished over the house,
And you have sworn off four nights of sleep,
And I have wrestled with a mind of airplanes and birth,
And to know that you are leaving again in the morning,
With me staying—or is it the other way around,
Me leaving, and you staying, or both of us
Boarding another flight to a strange city?
—And always, too, both of us wondering
If any of this exists,
                sleep, skies, birth,
Mumbling in the frontiers of hotel rooms,
Hauling our slender passports.
Plus: Speaking in forgotten tongues
Made up from the peasant poems of the Jews
And the soft-feathered hymns of the Cherokee.
And you so happy when we strolled through
The Dixie Classic Fair that autumn day
                in Forsyth County, North Carolina,
Because the caramel apples were made by hand,
And the tender pigs raced so hard
Around the swine track for their cookie,
And the blue ribbon chestnuts and sunflower seeds
Lay in their trays like hearts,
And the ladies from First Baptist
                serving fried tomatoes
Whispered to us
That we must avoid the brownies but it's OK
To eat the sweet potato pie,

And then, all day, not one Carolinian
Stopped us to talk about the trophies of eternity.
But, remember, all of this does exist —
Including the windy Moravian spires
And the dazzling bright Sunday hats,
Including the creeping lawns trimmed out to the roads,
Including the Avenue of the Arts
                              unzipping after dark
With its four-colored roosters
And fried chicken on Trade Street
And secret marriages
And the bronze whiskey at Finnegan's Pub
Brought over by svelte girls with shaved heads —
And the two of us exhausted with drink
                              and, finally, quiet,
So quiet, as if we could hear clarity
Bobble up from the bottom of the earth, so quiet,
Lushly quiet, leaf-by-murmuring-leaf quiet,
And now home,
Home in our own room, a nest
Above the garden's light, and waking.

POSTSCRIPT

The recipients of these epistolary poems include family, writers, friends, and friendly political rivals. They are composed in variable iambics with irregular rhyming. The letters cover the years 2007–2011, which correspond with the end of the Bush years and the beginning of the Obama era.

During that period, I traveled across the United States on over a hundred domestic flights covering some 200,000 miles. The stimulus for writing the poems often corresponded to an aural echo between the name of the recipient and the place name of my location, such as Plumly and Lummi, Buckley and Berkeley, Conda and Anaconda, C. D. and D.C. Readers should make little of this coincidence except to note the silly musical ear of the poet.

THE EPIGRAPHS

Sources for the epigraphs include *Pleasures and Regrets,* by Marcel Proust; "Those Corridors," by Czeslaw Milosz; "To My Brothers," by John Keats; and *Postcards from Ed,* by Edward Abbey.

TO _____ FROM THE JEWISH CEMETERY IN WILLIAMSON, WEST VIRGINIA

My wife—Wendy Willis, a former federal public defender for the District of Oregon, a leader in the field of civic engagement, and author of the collection of poems *Blood Sisters of the Republic*—and I had traveled to Williamson, where she met with the mayor, local activists, and elected officials who are working to reinvent the town's economy in ways that do not exclusively rely on the coal industry. We were in Williamson for two nights. Then we drove through the hollows of Mingo County on Highway 52 to spend some time in Blacksburg, Virginia, to celebrate our wedding anniversary.

TO WENDY FROM YELLOW HICKORY

For several years, even after we married, Wendy and I lived with our kids in two very small houses next door to each other on Hickory Street in the Ladd's

Addition neighborhood of Portland, Oregon. My house was named "Yellow Hickory" because it was painted yellow. Her house, painted white, was known as "Her Royal Hickory."

TO PLUMLY FROM LUMMI ISLAND

Poet Stanley Plumly has been a mentor and friend of mine since 1988, when I took his Form and Theory class at the University of Maryland. — Lummi Island is the most northeasterly of the San Juan archipelago. Located near Bellingham, Washington, it is served by a small ferry that makes the six-minute crossing about once an hour. It is two hours from Seattle, and one-and-a-half hours from Vancouver, B.C. — The Lummi Nation are a tribe of the Coast Salish. The tribe primarily resides on and around the Lummi Indian Reservation. The Lummi were forcibly moved to reservation lands after the signing of the Point Elliott Treaty in 1855.

TO HUGO FROM SODO

Poet Richard Hugo was born in White Center, Washington, in 1922. He lived in and around Seattle, served as a bombardier in World War II, played semi-pro baseball, worked for a short time as a technical writer at Boeing, and later taught creative writing at the University of Montana. He died in 1982. His book of epistolary poems, *31 Letters and 13 Dreams*, is a staple of Northwest literature. SoDo refers to south of downtown, an industrial neighborhood in Seattle. It is the location of Safeco Field, home of the Seattle Mariners.

TO BIESPIEL FROM SCHUL

"Adon Olam" has been a regular part of the daily Jewish liturgy since the 15th century and is typically sung to conclude sabbath and morning services. The title has been translated to mean "Eternal Lord."

TO WIMAN FROM WALLA WALLA

Poet Christian Wiman (CW) grew up in West Texas. We met in 1993 as Stegner Fellows at Stanford. — Walla Walla, Washington, is the home of poet Katrina Roberts, who teaches at Whitman College. Wendy and I had driven some six hours from Portland to have dinner with CW, who had given a reading the night before. We then stayed over for breakfast at Katrina's four-acre winery, Tytonidae. This was in the early spring of 2008, a few years after CW's first cancer diagnosis.

TO KELLER FROM SKAMANIA LODGE
TO RUEST FROM WINSTON-SALEM
TO GIFFORD FROM KIOWA COUNTY

Living in Boston in the mid-1980s, Nick Keller, Paul Ruest, Rick Gifford, and I created Glenville Productions, a loose group of activists, artists, educators, musicians, and writers. Keller is now a conservationist in Washington, D.C. Ruest is the principal and production director of the Argot Studios in New York City. Gifford teaches at the Conway Grammar School and is the founder of 12 Mile Meal in Northampton, Massachusetts.

TO BIERDS FROM THE CANNERY PIER HOTEL

Poet Linda Bierds teaches at the University of Washington and is the editor of the Pacific Northwest Poetry Series. She lives on Bainbridge Island. Some of the italicized words and phrases are borrowed from her poems. — The Cannery Pier Hotel is in Astoria, Oregon, the oldest American city west of the Rockies. The hotel was built on the site of the former Union Fish Cannery and extends some 600 feet into the Columbia River. — The poem was composed in April 2009, when U.S. Navy snipers fatally shot three Somali pirates who were holding hostage the captain of an American cargo ship.

TO ANSEL FROM THE HOTEL ANDRA

Talvikki Ansel is an American poet. We met in 1993 as Stegner Fellows at Stanford. — The Hotel Andra is in downtown Seattle, and Wendy and I like to stay there when we hole up in Seattle to write. The Andra is a stylish hipster hotel, but were you to meet Wendy and me, you would immediately spot that we're not hipsters.

TO DI PIERO FROM DUFUR

Poet W. S. Di Piero (Simone) is an essayist, translator, art critic, mentor, and friend. He grew up in Philadelphia and now lives in San Francisco. — Founded in 1907, the Balch Hotel in Dufur, Oregon, is now operated by Jeff and Samantha Irwin.

TO FARNSWORTH FROM BAR AVIGNON

Robert Farnsworth is a carpenter who lives in Machias, Maine. We met in 1990 when we were both living in Washington, D. C., in the Freud Hilton, an apartment building on Connecticut Avenue directly across from the National Zoo. It is called the Freud Hilton because for decades it housed more psychiatrists, psychologists, and clinical social workers than any other building in the District. — Bar Avignon is a wine bar on Portland's Division Street operated by Randy Goodman and Nancy Hunt. — For a word about Jeff Smith, see the note on "To Smith from Northampton."

TO COLLIER FROM UNITED FLIGHT 304

Since 1994, poet Michael Collier has been the director of the Bread Loaf Writer's Conference in Middlebury, Vermont. His sister Jeannie Collier was a member of the 1964 U.S. Olympic Diving Team. — From 1971 to 1986, I was a competitive springboard and platform diver. I competed in the U.S. Diving Championships against Olympic legend Greg Louganis and others. He beat me. By a lot. In the late 1990s, I coached elite divers, including several national and international champions.

TO BUCKLEY FROM BERKELEY

Founder and editor of the *National Review,* political writer, and critic William F. Buckley, Jr., was called the "scourge of liberalism" by Arthur M. Schlesinger, Jr., and was, in every conceivable way, the father of the contemporary conservative movement in the United States. — Berkeley, California, on the east side of San Francisco Bay, is one of the most liberal cities in America. — The "fat insurance man from Hartford" refers to Wallace Stevens, from whose poems some words and phrases have been borrowed.

TO CONDA FROM ANACONDA

From 2008 to 2010, Cesar Conda and I debated politics as daily contributors to *Politico.* Cesar has been instrumental in developing conservative policies in Washington, D.C. since the 1980s. From 2001 to 2003, Cesar served as assistant for domestic policy to Vice President Dick Cheney. He stopped writing for *Politico* in 2011, when he became chief of staff for Senator Marco Rubio (R-Florida). — The town of Anaconda, population ca. 9,000, is in southwest Montana. The Anaconda smelter stack is one of the tallest masonry structures in the world. When the Atlantic Richfield Company closed the smelter in 1980, it brought to an end almost a century of mineral processing in Anaconda. Today, an 18-hole golf course in the town, designed by Jack Nicklaus, uses the contaminated black slag from the smelter as the "sand" in the sand traps. — Wendy and I traveled through Montana for several days with Daniel Kemmis, who served both as mayor of Missoula and speaker of the Montana House of Representatives. While Dan and Wendy were meeting with Anaconda's civic leaders, I wandered into the Locker Room Bar, owned by Wendy's brother-in-law's father. I had never before met him, but he gave me a tour of the town in his Jeep. All told, we spent about three hours in Anaconda before driving to Bozeman. — The joke told in the poem is pure Dan.

TO WENDY FROM THE GERSHWIN HOTEL

The Gershwin Hotel is in Midtown Manhattan. The lyrics quoted from "How Long Has This Been Going On?" were written by Ira Gershwin. The song, composed by his brother, George, for the 1928 musical *Funny Face,* was introduced instead in the 1928 musical *Rosalie.*

TO SMITH FROM NORTHAMPTON

Artist Jeff Smith, a cohort of Glenville Productions in Boston during the 1980s, is a prominent member of the Fort Point Arts Community in the South End. He is best known for his "rolling sculptures" and two-dimensional recycled-wood mosaics, and I believe he can sometimes be found in the tonier neighborhoods and suburbs of Boston on garbage-pickup night, looking to secure found objects for his art projects. — Six times I have tried to visit Emily Dickinson's house in Amherst. Six times it has been closed.

TO SNYDER FROM THE BLUE SCORCHER CAFÉ

Gary Snyder is an American poet. — Some of the words and phrases in this poem are borrowed from or allude to Richard Hugo's poem "Letter to Snyder from Montana." — The Blue Scorcher Café, a worker-owned collective in Astoria, Oregon, is on the east side of downtown in the historic Fort George building. — The "Ursula" in the poem is writer Ursula K. Le Guin, who, along with Snyder and ecologist Jerry Franklin, participated in a panel discussion and reading at the First Baptist Church in Southwest Portland on May 18, 2010, to commemorate the 30th anniversary of the eruption of Mount St. Helens.

TO SYLVESTER FROM TERMINAL B

Artist and guitar-maker Phil Sylvester founded the Drawing Studio in Portland. He was the staff artist for *Poetry Northwest* from 2005 to 2010. His portraits and writings are featured in my book *Every Writer Has a Thousand Faces.* — When he attended Andover in 1969 as a teenager, Phil was roommates with future Florida governor Jeb Bush. — Houston Intercontinental Airport opened in 1969, a year after my family arrived in Texas from Oklahoma. In 1997, the airport was renamed the George Bush Intercontinental Airport to honor

George H. W. Bush, the forty-first president of the United States. The quotations from the Bush diary are from *The Presidents Club,* by Nancy Gibbs and Michael Duffy. — When I commuted between Portland and Winston-Salem, North Carolina, during the fall semesters of 2007 to 2011, I often had a layover in my hometown airport. Several times I bumped into childhood friends. — "Leaving on a Jet Plane" was written by John Denver in 1966 and became a popular single in 1969 by the folk trio Peter, Paul, and Mary.

TO C. D. FROM D.C.

C. D. Wright is a poet from Baxter County, Arkansas, who now lives in Providence, Rhode Island. — Some words and phrases are borrowed from the letters and poems of John Keats. — Whitey's Steak and Seafood reportedly closed in 2011.

TO UNRAU FROM UNION

Photographer Don Unrau grew up in northeast Montana and now lives in Portland, Oregon. He served as a medic in the U.S. Army during the Vietnam war. His first photographs of Vietnam were taken with a small Japanese rangefinder he carried as a soldier. Since 1982 he has created, shown, and published his seminal photographs of American and Viet Cong veterans in both the U.S. and Vietnam. — Clyde Gum, Jr., was elected commissioner of Monroe County in November 2010 with 54 percent of the vote.

TO LENNEY FROM THE GREENBRIER HOTEL

Dinah Lenney is an American writer and actress who lives in Los Angeles. — The Greenbrier was built in 1778 and is a National Historic Landmark. It was the site of the composition of the White Sulphur Manifesto, written in 1868 under the leadership of former Confederate general Robert E. Lee. The manifesto expresses the South's desire for reunification and restoration. The Greenbrier was also the secret location of the former U.S. Government Relocation Facility, known as the Bunker. The emergency shelter, which is now a tourist destination, is a massive underground facility that was built during the Cold War to house Congress in the event of a nuclear attack. In 2010, while spending a few days on holiday in nearby Greenville, West Virginia, Wendy and I, after a day of writing, wandered into the Greenbrier during their cocktail hour. As the dinner hour approached, so did formality: coat and tie for men, stockings and heels for women. We were severely underdressed and quietly slipped away.

TO LUKE FROM UNITED FLIGHT 251

My son Lucas Biespiel, a singer-songwriter and violinist, is currently a student at the Berklee College of Music in Boston.—The lyrics to "Love in Vain," quoted in the poem, are by Robert Johnson.

TO WENDY FROM THE CROW'S NEST

Crow's Nest is the name of the house Wendy and I now live in with our family. Located near Laurelhurst Park in the Sunnyside neighborhood of Portland, the Crow's Nest was built in 1915, the same year as the 40-acre park across the road that was designed in accordance with the plan of Frederick Law Olmsted, whose achievements in park design are too numerous to name. In 1919, the Pacific Coast Parks Association hailed the park as the "most beautiful park" on the West Coast. It is the first city park in the United States to be listed on the National Register of Historic Places.—The Dixie Classic Fair in Winston-Salem, North Carolina, began as a grain exposition in 1882.

ACKNOWLEDGMENTS

My gratitude to the editors of the following periodicals for first publishing some of the poems in this book:

Alhambra: "To Wendy from Yellow Hickory"
The Awl: "To Wendy from the Crow's Nest"
Boston Review: "To Conda from Anaconda"
Poetry International: "To Collier from United Flight 304"
Poetry Northwest: "To Hugo from SoDo," "To Luke from United Flight 251,"
    "To Plumly from Lummi Island"
Portland Review: "To Farnsworth from Bar Avignon"
The Rumpus: "To Biespiel from United Flight 1037"
TAB: The Journal of Poetry and Poetics: "To Keller from Skamania Lodge"
Zyzzyva: "To Unrau from Union"

ABOUT *the* AUTHOR

David Biespiel was born in 1964 in Tulsa, Oklahoma and grew up in Harris County, Texas, in Houston. A competitive springboard and platform diver from the age of seven, he competed in the NCCA as well as in the United States Diving Championships against Olympians Greg Louganis and Bruce Kimball, and later coached many regional and national divers. In 1999, he founded the Attic Institute, a literary think tank in Portland, Oregon.

In addition to writing, since 2003, the poetry column in the *Oregonian*, which is the longest-running newspaper column about poetry in the United States; serving as editor of *Poetry Northwest* from 2005 to 2010; being a regular contributor to *Politico* from 2008 to 2012; serving as a juror and board member for the National Book Critics Circle since 2010; and since 2012 writing the Poetry Wire blog for the *Rumpus*, he has published over a half a dozen books, including four volumes of poetry— *Shattering Air, Pilgrims & Beggars, Wild Civility,* and *The Book of Men and Women,* which was named one of the Best Books of the Year in 2009 by the Poetry Foundation—and a book on creativity, *Every Writer Has a Thousand Faces.* For his writing he has been awarded a National Endowment for the Arts Fellowship in Literature, a Stegner Fellowship at Stanford University, a Lannan Marfa residency, the Oregon Book Award, and the Pacific Northwest Booksellers Award.

Educated at Boston University, University of Maryland, and Stanford University, he has taught at colleges and universities throughout the United States, including the George Washington University, Stanford University, University of Maryland, Mount Vernon College, Lynchburg College as the Richard H. Thornton Writer in Residence, and Wake Forest University, where he was Poet in Residence from 2007 to 2011. He currently teaches in the Rainier Writing Workshop at Pacific Lutheran University, at Oregon State University, and at the Attic Institute. He lives in Portland.